The Pitman Motorists' Library

The Book of the
TRIUMPH HERALD, SPITFIRE and VITESSE

A Practical Handbook covering all models up to January 1970, including the Courier Van

Staton Abbey, M.I.M.I.

Pitman Publishing

First published 1961
Second edition 1964
Third edition 1967
Fourth edition 1970

SIR ISAAC PITMAN AND SONS LTD
Pitman House, Parker Street, Kingsway, London, W.C.2
P.O. Box 6038, Portal Street, Nairobi, Kenya

SIR ISAAC PITMAN (AUST.) PTY LTD
Pitman House, Bouverie Street, Carlton, Victoria 3053, Australia

PITMAN PUBLISHING COMPANY S.A. LTD
P.O. Box 9898, Johannesburg, S. Africa

PITMAN PUBLISHING CORPORATION
6 East 43rd Street, New York, N.Y. 10017, U.S.A.

SIR ISAAC PITMAN (CANADA) LTD
Pitman House, 381–383 Church Street, Toronto, 3, Canada

THE COPP CLARKE PUBLISHING COMPANY
517 Wellington Street, Toronto, 2B, Canada

ISBN 0 273 31417 3

Made in Great Britain at the Pitman Press, Bath
G0—(G.4186)

Preface

In planning this practical handbook it was necessary to bear in mind the needs not only of the novice, but also of the more technically-minded owner who would expect to carry out more ambitious work than that covered by the normal instruction book.

A considerable amount of supplementary material has, therefore, been included: decarbonizing and top-overhauls, and practical work on the ignition, carburation and braking systems, to take typical examples. Where special service tools and equipment are essential, however, it is pointed out that such jobs are obviously the province of a Standard-Triumph dealer.

It is hoped that the book will be of real value to "do-it-yourself" owners; some may, perhaps, be willing to pass on further practical hints and tips for the benefit of other readers. In this respect, it is necessary to acknowledge gratefully the assistance given by Standard-Triumph Sales, Ltd., in supplying information and many of the illustrations used in this book.

STATON ABBEY

Creek House
St. Osyth
Essex

Contents

1 Maintenance and Running Adjustments

Do-it-yourself owners who have graduated to the Herald, Spitfire or Vitesse from earlier types of car will find that routine maintenance has been considerably simplified by the use, wherever possible, of rubber-bushed or nylon bearings in the steering and suspension linkages. Greasing points are confined to the steering swivels, the water pump and the front and rear wheel hubs.

In earlier handbooks the various jobs are grouped under 3,000-mile, 6,000-mile and 12,000-mile headings. These recommendations were later amended, however; the 3,000-mile service was deleted and the jobs falling due at this mileage were combined with those to be done under the 6,000-mile heading. The maintenance summary on page 2 is based broadly on this later scheme.

An owner who carries out most of the work himself, however, may find it an advantage to draw up a chart of the various jobs on a week-to-week basis, appropriate to the average mileage covered, instead of devoting a week-end to, say, the 12,000-mile service; it is largely a matter of individual preference and convenience.

Very little equipment is required for home servicing, other than the usual collection of spanners, screwdrivers, pliers, feeler gauges and so on which are to be found in the average handyman's garage. A grease gun is, of course, necessary and access to the underside of the car is made much easier—and safer—if a pair of drive-on wheel ramps is used, or failing these, a pair of adjustable axle stands. Never rely on the jack alone to support the car when working beneath it.

A starting handle is not provided as standard. The easiest method of turning the engine when carrying out adjustments is to remove all the sparking plugs (to relieve the pistons of compression) and to rotate the crankshaft either by pulling on the fan belt or by engaging top gear and inching the car forward.

The real answer to the problem, however, is to invest in an ingenious device known as the Junior Autopoints Unit, which is obtainable from Eldred Motors and Electronics Ltd., 855 Holderness Road, Hull, E. Yorks. When this is connected-up to the battery and starter soleniod switch, the engine can be inched round at the slowest possible speed, making precise adjustment an easy matter.

A very useful lubrication chart suitable for hanging on the garage wall can be obtained, free of charge, from the Castrol Chart Library, Castrol

House, Marylebone Road, London, N.W.1. Simply drop them a postcard mentioning this book and the year and model of your car.

MAINTENANCE SUMMARY
EVERY 6,000 MILES
or every 6 months (whichever occurs first)

1. *Engine:* Drain oil and refill (normal service—*see* page 9).
2. *Carburettors:* Service air cleaner. Top-up piston dashpots (twin-carburettor engines).
3. *Brake and clutch master cylinders:* Top-up fluid levels. Check pipes and unions for fluid leakage.
4. *Battery:* Top-up cells with distilled water.
5. *Shock absorbers:* Check for leakage.
6. *Tyre pressures:* Check.
7. *Wheel nuts:* Check tightness.
8. *Engine:* Check and adjust valve clearances.
9. *Engine lubrication:* Clean filter in oil filler cap.
10. *Steering Lower Swivels:* Remove plug, fit nipple and lubricate.
11. *Control joints, door hinges and locks:* Lubricate.
12. *Sparking plugs:* Clean and adjust.
13. *Ignition distributor:* Lubricate and service.
14. *Fan and dynamo driving belt:* Check tension; adjust if necessary.
15. *Petrol pump:* Clean filter.
16. *Clutch:* Check free movement. Adjust and bleed hydraulic system if necessary.
17. *Front wheel alignment and balance:* Have check made by dealer.
18. *Wheels and Tyres:* Check for damage and flints. Change round to equalize tyre wear.
19. *Handbrake cables:* Check for fraying; lubricate around guides.

EVERY 12,000 MILES
or every 12 months (whichever occurs first)

Carry out items 1–19 and following additional work—

20. *Engine Lubrication:* Fit new oil filter.
21. *Gearbox and rear axle:* Top-up oil levels.
22. *Rear suspension:* Lubricate hubs. Spray or paint springs with oil.
23. *Steering gearbox:* Lubricate.
24. *Dynamo:* Lubricate.
25. *Carburettors:* Dismantle and clean. Re-set idling speed and mixture adjustments.
26. *Sparking plugs:* As a precaution, fit new plugs.
27. *Cooling system:* Descale, drain and flush.
28. *Engine:* Have compression and vacuum tests carried out by dealer.
29. *Water pump:* Lubricate.
30. *Front hubs:* Dismantle, check bearings and re-pack with grease.
31. *Crankcase breather valve (when fitted):* Dismantle and clean.

Every 24,000 miles or every 18 months

32. *Braking system:* Change hydraulic fluid.
33. *Braking system:* Renew all rubber seals and hoses.

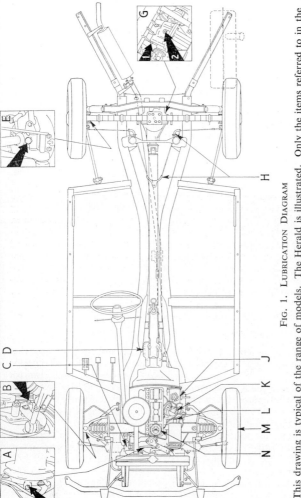

FIG. 1. LUBRICATION DIAGRAM

This drawing is typical of the range of models. The Herald is illustrated. Only the items referred to in the Maintenance Summary which require lubrication are shown.

A. Water pump
B. Lower steering swivels (both sides)
C. Steering unit
D. Gearbox
E. Rear hubs (both sides)
G. Rear axle: 1, filler and level plug.
    2, drain plug (not fitted to all models)

H. Handbrake cable guides
J. Oil cleaner
K. Ignition distributor
L. Generator rear bearing
M. Front wheel hubs (both sides)
N. Engine oil filler

In this chapter it is proposed to group, under the appropriate mileage headings, the items in the Maintenance Summary that call for a little further explanation but which can be carried out—even by a novice—with the tools likely to be found in the average home garage. Before dealing with these specific jobs, however, some general notes on maintenance points not covered by the summary may not be out of place. If some of the information seems to be rather elementary, the more experienced reader is asked to remember the needs of the novice.

Daily Inspections. Every morning, or before starting on a long run, it is advisable to check the engine-oil level with the dipstick. The level should, of course, be topped-up at intervals to bring the oil to the "full" mark. These checks should be made with the car standing on level ground and a short time should always be allowed for the oil to drain back into the crankcase; otherwise a misleading reading may be obtained.

The oil should not be allowed to fall below the danger mark on the dipstick or serious damage may be caused. If the engine is in good condition, topping-up should be needed only every 200 or 300 miles, or at even longer periods when the engine is new; a worn engine, however, will need more frequent checks. Remember, too, that the oil consumption will be increased in hot weather and will be quite substantially increased when long, fast runs are undertaken, as compared with the figure that one becomes accustomed to when shorter runs at modest speeds are the order of the day. Tests have shown that the oil does not attain its maximum temperature until the car has been running for approximately one hour.

The level of the water in the radiator header tank should also be checked, as described on page 6.

Choice of Engine Oil. It should not be necessary to emphasize that "cheap" oils are the most expensive in the long run. Modern oils contain special additives which reduce corrosion of the cylinder walls, prevent the formation of sludge and gum and leave the engine in a very clean condition. Multigrade oils, which are rather more expensive than the standard grades, have the added advantage of remaining relatively "thin" even at freezing temperature, thus reducing oil drag during starting and ensuring instant lubrication of the cylinder walls: but at the same time they maintain sufficient viscosity or "body" at high temperatures to prevent damage when an engine is heavily loaded or is driven for long periods at high speeds.

The viscosity of the oil is indicated by a reference number. For example an SAE 20 or 20W oil is relatively fluid at low temperatures and a 10W oil more fluid still. SAE 30, 40 or 50 oils, on the other hand, are progressively "thicker" and retain their body better at high temperatures, although they will cause more drag when starting from cold and will be slower to circulate in a cold engine. Where only a single-viscosity oil is available, an SAE 20W grade should be used in temperate climates, SAE 30 in the sub-tropics and SAE 10W when arctic temperatures prevail. The multi-grade oils referred to earlier, however, offer a much more effective compromise. An oil which has a 20W/50 grading, for example, will be

FIG. 2. UNDER-BONNET VIEW OF HERALD

1. Windscreen wiper	9. Ignition distributor
2. Brake fluid reservoir	10. Dynamo (generator)
3. Clutch fluid reservoir	11. Water filler cap
4. Heater water valve	12. Oil-level dipstick
5. Interior heater casing	13. Thermostat housing
6. Battery	14. Oil filler cap
7. Ignition coil	15. Air intake filter
8. Starter switch	

suitable for all normal temperatures except arctic conditions (when a 10W/40 oil should be used).

When an engine is badly worn and a single-grade oil is in use, oil consumption can be reduced by choosing a heavier grade than that normally specified.

Oil-pressure Warning Light. Of equal importance is the green oil-pressure warning lamp which, like the ignition warning lamp, should be extinguished as soon as the engine is running, as the contacts on the switch mounted on the engine are designed to open when the oil pressure in the lubrication system exceeds 5–7 lb per sq in.

If the lamp continues to glow, the car should not be driven until the oil level in the sump has been checked. If all appears to be in order, and there is no sign of external leakage or clatter from the engine when it is cautiously speeded up, it is possible that the oil pressure-operated switch is faulty. Most garages will be able to test the switch and to check the pressure in the lubrication system by connecting a pressure gauge to the switch union. The normal running pressure at 40–50 m.p.h. is 40–60 lb per sq in.

Low Oil Pressure. If an oil-pressure gauge is fitted, a pressure of at least 40 lb per sq in. should be recorded when the engine is thoroughly warmed-up and running at a fairly fast speed; about 20 lb should be shown at idling speed. Incidentally, it is possible to fit an oil gauge and at the same time to retain the warning light if the oil-pressure switch is replaced by a special adaptor, to which the pressure gauge pipe can be connected.

Assuming that the sump is full and that the correct grade of oil is used, low oil pressure can be caused by a choked intake in the sump, a faulty oil-pressure relief valve or a worn pump.

Fortunately the pump is seldom at fault (except when the engine has covered a very large mileage). The oil-pressure relief valve is, however, a possible culprit. This valve, which relieves the excessive pressure that would otherwise be developed in the system when the oil is cold, is retained by a domed hexagon nut at the base of the distributor shaft tunnel on the left-hand side of the engine. The valve should be removed and cleaned. The seating in the block should also be cleaned with a lint-free cloth wrapped around the end of a length of wood. If the strength of the spring has weakened a new spring should be fitted. The valve is not adjustable.

If satisfactory pressure is not restored when the above points have been attended to, the crankshaft and connecting-rod bearings are probably badly worn.

Topping-up the Radiator. The water level in the radiator header tank should be checked regularly, although frequent topping-up should not be necessary. The filler cap is fitted with a spring-loaded valve that maintains a pressure in the system when the engine is hot, thus raising the boiling point and also preventing loss of water. It is bad practice to top-up the system when the engine is cold as this is likely to lead to un-necessary loss of water (and relatively expensive anti-freeze solution, when this is in use) as the water in the system expands when the engine warms up.

Owing to the pressure existing in the system when the water is hot, the cap should be wrapped in a cloth before it is removed and to avoid any risk of scalding it should be turned progressively to allow the pressure to escape before it is finally lifted off.

When a radiator-overflow bottle is provided (this is often termed a "sealed" cooling system), it is normally sufficient to make sure that the translucent reservoir is half-full. In cold weather it is advisable to use a mixture of equal quantities of water and anti-freezing compound in the bottle and to top-up with this mixture—not with plain water.

Anti-freezing Solutions. When there is any risk of the temperature falling below freezing point during the winter months, it is advisable to descale and flush-out the cooling system as described on pages 23–4 and to fill-up with an anti-freezing solution, rather than relying on the doubtful precaution of draining the system overnight. If an interior heater is fitted, in fact, it is essential to use anti-freeze, as the heater element cannot be drained completely by opening the radiator and cylinder-block drain taps.

Even when an engine heater is used the cooling system must, of course, be protected when the car is parked in the open. It is also possible for the radiator to freeze when the car is first driven away after a cold start, since the thermostat will prevent circulation of water from the engine until the normal running temperature is reached.

It is essential to use an ethylene-glycol solution containing suitable inhibitors to prevent the glycol corroding the metal in the cooling system. Any of the well-known brands will be quite satisfactory in this respect. The correct amount of anti-freeze to use will be stated on the container or in a leaflet or chart obtainable from the supplier. Generally, two pints, representing one part of anti-freeze to four parts of water, will give complete protection down to approximately 17°F (15 degrees of frost).

Beware of the statements issued by many suppliers that this proportion will give protection against 35 degrees of frost. While it is true that there will be no risk of a cracked block or a damaged radiator, the solution will have formed ice crystals and its "mushy" condition will prevent adequate flow through the system. When the thermometer drops to those levels the engine must be allowed to idle for at least five minutes after being started from cold, preferably with the radiator covered, to allow the system to warm up. In order to obtain complete protection at very low temperatures, in the neighbourhood of zero Fahrenheit, a mixture consisting of equal volumes of anti-freeze and water is required. This is a point that doctors and others who may wish to drive away from cold without delay should bear in mind.

It is always better to top-up with a solution rather than pure water. The anti-freeze ingredient in the solution itself does not evaporate, but when fairly frequent topping-up is needed it is obvious that the coolant must be escaping through a leak at some point. It is necessary to discover and cure the leak (*see* pages 24–5) and then add anti-freeze solution to prevent the remaining solution being unduly weakened.

Topping-up the Battery. The level of the electrolyte in the cells of the battery should not be allowed to fall below the tops of the separators or the separator guards. At least at monthly intervals—more frequently in hot weather, say once a week—a check should be made and *distilled* water should be added until this level is reached in each cell.

Never use tapwater or rainwater, which usually contains impurities that will shorten the life of the battery. The water that condenses in the drip tray of a refrigerator when the freezing coils are defrosted, however, can be used; but *not* water obtained by melting ice cubes!

Never use a naked flame when inspecting the level of the fluid in the cells, as an explosive mixture of hydrogen and oxygen may be present.

It is best to add water just before the cells are to be charged. In cold weather this will allow the acid and water to mix thoroughly and thus avoid any risk of the water freezing and damaging the plates and battery case. It should not be necessary to add acid unless some of the electrolyte has been spilt, in which case a Standard-Triumph dealer should be consulted. If acid is added in order to raise the specific gravity of the electrolyte, the plates may be damaged.

The need for excessive topping-up of all the cells is usually an indication of an unduly high generator charging rate. If one cell regularly requires more water than the others, a leak in that cell must be suspected. Even a slow leak may, in time, completely drain the acid from a cell.

Remember that the electrolyte is a solution of sulphuric acid in water and is very corrosive. Never place the vent plugs on the bodywork. If any electrolyte is spilled, wipe it away immediately with a clean wet cloth and then dry the part thoroughly; household ammonia, if available, will neutralize the acid.

Steering Column Adjustment. The Herald is unusual among moderately-priced cars in having provision for adjustment of the length of the steering column, thus allowing the steering wheel to be set to give the most comfortable driving position.

A further refinement is that the telescopic joint in the column will collapse if the driver is thrown violently against the steering wheel in an accident, preventing serious injury to the chest which so often occurs in these circumstances. As this valuable protection depends on the correct tensioning of the clamping bolts on the telescopic joint, it is advisable to use a torque-indicating wrench when tightening them. It is preferable, therefore, to leave the adjustment of the steering wheel to a Standard-Triumph dealer. When this is not possible, the clamping nuts on earlier cars or the set-screw which is recessed to take an Allen wrench on later models, should be tightened firmly but not over-tightened. Before the column can be adjusted it may also be necessary to slacken the upper and lower brackets. After adjustment, tighten these nuts firmly.

Jacking the Car. The scissor-type jack is retained by the strap in the luggage compartment, next to the petrol tank. By rotating the central screw by hand the jack can be expanded sufficiently to hold it securely in position.

In order to raise the car, position the jack beneath one of the body-mounting bolts in the corner of the chassis frame, just in front of a rear wheel or behind a front wheel, as the case may be. Do not be tempted to jack at any other point, owing to the risk of distorting the chassis or body. The squared end of the jack handle engages with the socket on the end of the central screw and the bar in the tool kit (which has a hooked end that is used to lever-off the hub plates) is passed through the outer end of the handle in order to turn it.

Check that the handbrake is fully applied and that the car is on firm, level ground. If a wheel that is to be removed is next to the kerb, make sure that there will be sufficient space to allow it to be drawn off its studs when it has been jacked-up.

THE 6,000-MILE SERVICE

The work to be carried out at this stage is quite straightforward. The following notes on some of the items listed in the Maintenance Summary should clear up any difficulties that might be experienced by the novice.

Changing the Engine Oil. The engine oil becomes contaminated with carbon and other products of combustion, including condensed water and fuel, and must, therefore, be drained out at least at 6,000-mile intervals. If the engine is worn, the degree of gas leakage past the piston rings may make it advisable to change the oil more frequently; for example, it is usually recommended that a change at 3,000 miles shows some economy in the long run, since, by maintaining the quality of the oil, the overall consumption is reduced. Also, more frequent changes are advisable when most of the driving is done in cold weather, particularly when frequent starts are made from cold and when the engine is allowed to idle for long periods. At the other extreme, in hot, dusty conditions the oil will deteriorate more quickly than in temperate climates.

The oil should be drained when the car has just come in from a run; being hot, it will be more fluid and will be holding in suspension the impurities that have accumulated.

If a modern premium oil is used, it should not be necessary to flush out the sump with flushing oil, as was often recommended with older types of car. As the sump may contain up to seven pints of oil, a sufficiently large drain pan should be provided. An old kitchen washing-up bowl is a useful container for this purpose. Sufficient time should be allowed for the oil to drain completely before the drain plug is replaced. The sump should then be refilled until the level is up to the "full" mark on the dipstick.

Topping-up Gearbox and Rear Axle Oil Levels. A gear oil that has an "extreme-pressure" additive should be used for the gearbox and rear axle, the same grade being suitable for winter and summer running. Such oils can be identified by the letters EP or XP or GX before the viscosity figure.

As the combined filler and level plugs are at the sides of the gearbox and axle casings, it is rather an awkward job to inject oil unless a piece of rubber tubing is fitted to the spout of a forced-feed oil can. Alternatively, the Castrol "Handi-pack," which has a transparent flexible feed tube, fills the bill admirably. Oil should be injected until it begins to overflow

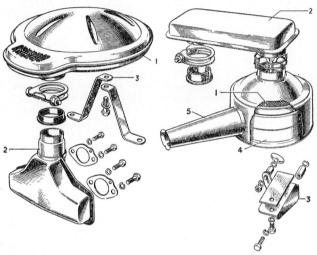

FIG. 3. GAUZE-TYPE AIR CLEANER (*left*) AND OIL-BATH TYPE (*right*)

1. Cleaner element
2. Air duct
3. Bracket
4. Oil bath
5. Air intake extension

from the filler hole. Wait until the drips have stopped before refitting the plug.

When an overdrive is fitted, this is lubricated automatically from the gearbox. Topping up the oil level of the gearbox will therefore automatically correct the level in the overdrive housing.

If there is no evidence of leakage from the gearbox and rear axle, a check on the oil levels can be deferred until the 12,000-mile service.

Servicing Carburettor Air Cleaner. The mileage at which the air cleaner needs attention will depend, of course, on the conditions under which the car is driven. In dusty conditions it will need more frequent attention, but 6,000 miles is normally the mileage at which the air cleaner should be serviced. The dust should be lightly brushed off a pleated-paper type of air cleaner. If the element is very dirty, renew it.

The gauze type of filter should be cleaned by swilling the gauze element

FIG. 4. PLEATED-PAPER AIR FILTERS
Left, Herald.   *Right*, earlier Vitesse.

A flange mounting is used on the later Heralds. The later Vitesse models and the Spitfire have two pleated-paper elements in a single container

thoroughly in paraffin. After allowing the element to dry, dip the gauze in clean engine oil and shake off the surplus oil.

The oil-bath type air cleaner can be cleaned by removing the air duct, unscrewing the wing nut at the top of the cleaner and lifting the cover and filter unit from the body of the filter. Empty the oil and clean out any accumulation of sludge. The filter should be washed in petrol and the air cleaner body filled with fresh engine oil up to the level of the arrow.

Topping-up Carburettor Dashpots. This attention is required only on twin-carburettor engines which are fitted with S.U. or Zenith-Stromberg carburettors. Remove the air cleaner, unscrew the cap-nut from the top of each suction chamber and carefully withdraw the small plunger. This contains a one-way valve and checks the upward movement of the piston, thus preventing the piston rising too quickly when the throttle is suddenly

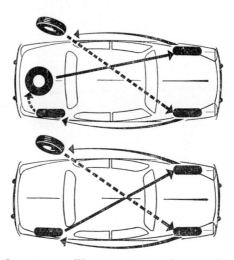

FIG. 5. CHANGING THE WHEELS AROUND TO EQUALIZE TYRE WEAR
The upper method brings the spare wheel into use

opened. This would cause an unduly weak mixture. The hydraulic damper also prevents the piston "fluttering" under certain running conditions.

The oil chamber in the piston rod must therefore be kept full of engine oil (SAE 20W/50). Usually it is sufficient to top-up at 3,000-mile intervals but, if the carburettor is worn, more frequent topping-up may be required—possibly every 1,000 miles. On no account use thin machine oil, which is suitable only to lubricate the piston rods of earlier types of S.U. carburettor which had no oil dashpot. The point is stressed because some garage mechanics do not seem to be aware of the distinction. If the performance is sluggish or "spitting back" occurs when the throttle is suddenly opened and the engine is at its normal operating temperature, check that the right grade of oil has been used in the dashpot.

Brake and Clutch Fluid Reservoirs. These are in the engine compartment. Wipe the caps and sides perfectly clean before unscrewing the caps to check the fluid levels. Top-up if necessary to within $\frac{1}{4}$ in. of the top of each reservoir, using Castrol Girling Brake and Clutch fluid or, if this is not available, any alternative fluid which conforms to the specification SAE 70R3.

Tyre Pressure Checks. It is essential to use an accurate pressure gauge when checking the tyre pressures (which are listed in Chapter 7) and to protect it from knocks and grit when it is not in use. Garage airline gauges are not always accurate. The conscientious owner may

FIG. 6. ADJUSTING THE TAPPETS

take a tip from rally and competition drivers, who generally use the pocket dial-type of gauge in preference to the extending type. The Aerite gauge made by Walters and Dobson of Sheffield is an excellent example.

Whenever pressures are checked, make sure that the valve caps are replaced and tightened firmly. These are intended to prevent leakage and at the same time exclude mud, grit and ice from the relatively vulnerable inner seals. If a cap should be lost a replacement should be fitted as soon as possible.

If the tyres are fitted with inner tubes, pressure will be lost at the rate of from 1 to 3 lb per week, owing to a process known as "diffusion."

Oxygen from the air in the tyre is absorbed by the rubber and a corresponding amount of oxygen is given off from the outer surface of the tube. It is necessary, therefore, to restore this slight loss of pressure even when the tubes are in first-class condition. Synthetic rubber tubes and tubeless tyres do not suffer from this disadvantage but it is still advisable to check the pressures regularly.

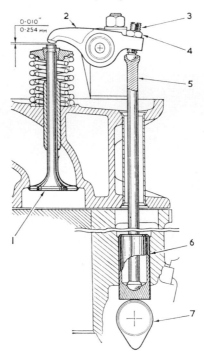

FIG. 7. THE VALVE OPERATING MECHANISM

1. Valve	5. Push-rod
2. Rocker	6. Tappet
3. Adjusting screw	7. Cam
4. Lock-nut	

Valve Clearance Adjustment. If a highly-efficient overhead-valve engine is to be kept in good tune it is essential to check the valve clearances at 6,000-mile intervals. The correct clearance between the tips of the inlet and exhaust valves and the rockers, when the valve is closed and the tappet is on the base of the cam, is 0·010 in. (10 thousandths of an inch) with the engine cold.

To make sure that each tappet is on the base of the cam, turn the engine until the valve to be adjusted has just closed and then give the crankshaft a further half-turn.

If a starting handle is not provided, remove the sparking plugs and rotate the engine by pulling on the fan belt.

To adjust the clearance, slacken off the adjusting-screw lock-nut at the opposite end of the rocker to the valve and insert an accurate feeler blade between the toe of the rocker and the valve tip. The adjusting screw should now be turned with a screwdriver until the correct clearance is obtained and held in this position while the lock-nut is tightened. A firm pressure should be applied to the screwdriver in order to displace all but a thin film of oil from the cupped ends of the tappet and push rod. A false clearance may otherwise be obtained. Tighten the lock-nut and re-check the clearance.

The action of tightening the lock-nut will usually be found to change the adjustment slightly, so that one or two attempts may be necessary before an accurate clearance is obtained. It is advisable to use two feeler gauges to check the adjustment—one 0·001 in. too large, which should not enter, and one 0·001 in. too small, which should enter easily.

Remember that if the cylinder-head nuts are tightened down, the clearances will be reduced.

Before replacing the valve rocker cover inspect the cover gasket. If there is any doubt regarding its condition it should be renewed. Make sure that the cover is seating evenly on the cylinder head and is located correctly over the studs, before replacing the fibre washers and tightening the securing nuts evenly.

Lubricating Lower Steering Swivels. The lower swivel-bearings that carry the front-wheel stub-axles must be lubricated with hypoid gear oil—not grease. The plug fitted to each swivel-bearing must be unscrewed and replaced by a grease nipple to allow oil to be pumped into the bearing until it exudes from the flange. The grease nipple can then be removed and the plug replaced, or the nipple left in place until the next service—which would seem to be the most sensible course.

Oilcan Attentions. For oilcan lubrication of the various control joints, locks and hinges a good-quality light engine oil, or preferably an oil which has anti-rust properties, can be used. Another excellent lubricant is an upper-cylinder oil such as Redex, which tends to prevent gumming.

On parts such as door hinges and catches, surplus oil should be wiped off to prevent soiling of driver's or passenger's clothes. A solidified lubricant can be obtained for this purpose which is rather cleaner than ordinary oil or the lock tongues and catch-plates can be rubbed with a wax candle.

Keep the Plugs Clean. A smoothly running engine, good "tick-over," easy starting, and a full power output, depend to a large extent on the sparking plugs, which require regular attention if engine efficiency is to be maintained. This attention involves keeping the plugs clean and the electrode gaps correctly adjusted. In the ordinary way examine the plugs every few thousand miles. Note whether the insulators are sooted or oily. The plugs and the method of cleaning them and setting the gaps are dealt with in detail in Chapter 3.

Servicing the Ignition Distributor. The distributor cap should be removed, after springing aside the two securing clips. In most cases the rotor, which is attached to the top of the cam spindle, can be pulled off fairly easily by hand. If it is tight, it should be eased off by rocking it slightly from side to side as a firm upward pull is applied.

When the rotor has been removed a small screw which secures the cam will be revealed. A few drops of light oil should be placed on this screw, as a space is provided between the screw threads to allow the oil to lubricate the interior of the distributor. A few drops of oil should also be applied through the opening in the distributor base plate, adjacent to the cam, to lubricate the governor-weight mechanism. Although engine oil may be used for this purpose a good upper-cylinder lubricant, such as Redex, is preferable. This type of oil tends to prevent gumming and also prevents the formation of rust.

A thin film of petroleum jelly should also be applied to the contact-breaker cam faces; this should be done sparingly owing to the risk of the lubricant finding its way on to the contact points.

It is a good plan at this stage to separate the points by pulling the moving arm back with the tip of the finger. The points should have a grey, frosted appearance; they should not be unduly burnt or pitted, although the formation of a slight "pip" on one point and a corresponding "crater" on the other is quite normal. Full information regarding servicing the points will be found in Chapter 3.

Check the Fan Belt Tension. The fan belt, which also drives the dynamo, should be kept free from grease and should be correctly tensioned. There should be a free movement of one inch at the centre of the belt. If the belt is too slack, it will slip; on the other hand, if it is too tightly adjusted, excessive wear will occur on the fan and generator bearings. It is a simple matter to adjust the tension by loosening the two upper mounting bolts on the generator and the clamping bolt on the strut, allowing the generator to be swung towards or away from the engine. To increase the tension on the belt, pull the generator outwards; do not use any leverage. After the mounting bolts have been tightened, re-check the free movement of the belt.

The belt must be kept free from grease or oil. If it develops a squeak or a whistle, dust it with French chalk or smear the edges with a little brake fluid.

When the time comes to renew the belt on the Herald and Spitfire it is worthwhile fitting a Ferodo belt instead of the Goodyear type which is fitted as standard. The Ferodo belt costs more, but is a little longer, thus

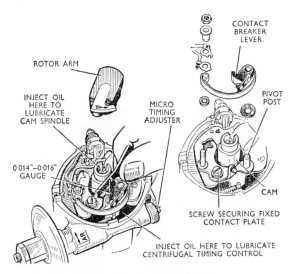

FIG. 8. DISTRIBUTOR SERVICE

When the moving contact arm (*right*) has been removed, the plate carrying the fixed contact can be taken off. A different method of clamping the spring is used on the Spitfire distributor.

allowing the dynamo to be swung further away from the cylinder block and making it much easier to remove and fit No. 1 sparking plug.

Cleaning Petrol Pump Filter. Undo the screw at the centre of the pump cover and remove the cover, the gasket and the screen or filter and swill the filter gauze in petrol. The sediment chamber in the pump collects impurities and water which may enter the pump.

Make sure, when replacing the cover, that the fibre washer is fitted beneath the head of the screw when the pump has a metal cover, that the gasket is not fractured and that the cover is bedding down properly.

Use a new gasket if in any doubt. An air leak at this gasket is one of the most common causes of pump failure.

Clutch Adjustment. On cars produced up to late 1960, an adjustment is provided to restore the free movement at the clutch pedal which is gradually taken up as the linings wear. On later cars, however, this adjustment

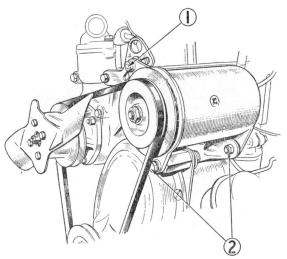

FIG. 9. FAN AND DYNAMO DRIVING BELT ADJUSTMENT
1. Adjustable strut   2. Pivot bolts

is unnecessary; the following instructions apply, therefore, only to earlier models. A free movement at the pedal of at least $\frac{1}{2}$ in. should be maintained by unhooking the return spring, releasing the lock-nut shown in Fig. 10 and screwing the adjusting nut along the rod until a 0·080 in. feeler gauge can be inserted between the nut and the bracket when the rod is pushed into the clutch housing by hand. Tighten the lock-nut and refit the return spring.

If the clutch does not free properly when the adjustment is correct, the trouble must lie at some point within the clutch mechanism and will call for specialist attention.

When clutch judder develops the most likely cause is worn or glazed friction linings, a defective centre-plate or internal release mechanism. If the pedal has a "spongy" action, it will be necessary to bleed air from the hydraulic system as described in Chapter 5, when dealing with the brakes. There is a bleed nipple on the clutch-operating cylinder.

Cases have been known in which renewal of the clutch driven plate has been necessary on the Herald after as little as 12,000 miles, but this can often be traced to abuse of the clutch, such as excessive slipping in order

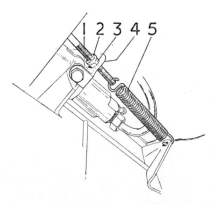

FIG. 10. CLUTCH ADJUSTMENT ON EARLY HERALDS

1. Adjusting rod
2. Lock-nut
3. Adjusting nut

4. Abutment bracket
5. Return spring

to avoid the necessity for changing to a lower gear, or the bad habit of using the clutch pedal as a rest for the left foot.

Check Front-wheel Alignment and Balance. When rapid tread wear occurs only on the front tyres, the alignment of the front wheels should be checked by a properly-equipped service station. Makeshift methods of adjustment at home are insufficiently accurate to suit modern independent suspension systems. Remember that an error in alignment of $\frac{1}{2}$ in. will have the same effect as dragging a tyre sideways for 87 feet in every mile on the road!

The other aspects of steering geometry are equally important and can be checked with modern precision equipment. Incorrect camber angle and swivel-pin inclination will cause more rapid wear on one side of the tyre than the other; driving on steeply-cambered roads, incidentally, will have the same effect.

An unbalanced wheel and tyre will cause a twisting, tramping action that can not only affect the steering and cause vibration, but also grinds rubber off the tyre tread and accelerates wear on the steering linkage and front suspension. Most larger garages nowadays have wheel-balancing equipment on which both static and dynamic balance can be checked and corrected quickly and at a modest cost.

Changing Tyres Around. Apart from regular pressure checks longer life can be obtained from a set of tyres by equalizing, as far as possible, the wear on the individual treads. This calls for changing the wheels around (preferably at 3,000-mile intervals). Fig. 5 shows alternative schemes, the choice depending on whether a reliable tyre is fitted to the spare wheel. At the same time examine the treads carefully and prise out any flints or other sharp objects.

Finally, remember that speed costs money: tyres wear twice as quickly at 65 m.p.h. as at 30 m.p.h., and fast cornering, rapid acceleration and heavy braking must all be paid for in terms of tread rubber.

THE 12,000-MILE SERVICE

The work to be done at this stage (in addition to the 6,000-mile items shown on the Maintenance Summary) is mainly concerned with lubrication,

FIG. 11. THE REPLACEABLE TYPE OF OIL FILTER

as detailed in the following notes. The cooling system should, however, be descaled and flushed out, as described below. The carburettor, or carburettors, will also benefit from a thorough servicing; this work is described in detail in Chapter 4.

When this has been done it is as well to have the condition of the engine checked systematically by a dealer who possesses vacuum and compression gauges and other specialized engine test-tune equipment.

Renewing the Oil Filter. The oil filter must be renewed at 6,000-mile intervals; otherwise there is a risk of unfiltered oil reaching the engine bearings. On the four-cylinder engines the filter takes the form of a replaceable cartridge which is simply unscrewed from the crankcase. Sometimes, however, a filter can be too tight to unscrew by hand and must be slackened by using a strap-wrench or by tapping it round with any suitable tool such as an old screwdriver.

Before screwing the replacement filter home, clean the joint faces and smear them with oil. Check for any signs of leakage after the engine has been running for a few minutes.

On the Vitesse, the filter element alone is replaced. The casing is retained by a central bolt. Clean out the interior of the casing thoroughly before installing the new filter and make sure that the flange of the casing seats properly on the crankcase before finally tightening the central bolt firmly. Run the engine and check for leakage at the flange or past the central bolt. It is possible to fit the wrong type of element on these engines —which would seriously restrict oil circulation—so make sure that the garage or Standard-Triumph dealer supplies you with the correct item, cross-checking against the latest parts list.

Water Pump Lubrication. The plug should be removed from the upper surface of the pump and a grease nipple fitted. Give only five strokes of the gun, using general-purpose grease. The plug can be refitted or the nipple left in place for convenience in subsequent servicing.

Topping-up Gearbox and Rear Axle. Although a check on the oil level in the gearbox and overdrive (when fitted) has been mentioned under the 6,000-mile heading, this job, and checking the level in the rear axle, can usually be deferred until the 12,000-mile service. Early instruction books call for draining and refilling the axle at this mileage but the improved lubricants which are available nowadays have rendered this job unnecessary (apart from the oil change which is carried out during the free service after the first 1,000 miles have been covered).

Lubricating the Rear Hubs. On the underside of each rear hub, beneath the driving shaft, is a plug which must be unscrewed to allow a grease nipple to be fitted. Inject grease until it exudes from the bearing. If the car is used in wet and muddy conditions, it would be better to lubricate the hubs every 6,000 miles—not necessarily to replace the grease, but to force out any grit. On some models there has been a history of rear hub bearing failure if lubrication has been neglected.

Lubricating Front Wheel Bearings. Jack up the front of the car and remove one front road wheel. When disc brakes are fitted, without disturbing the hydraulic pipe unions unscrew the caliper securing bolts and lift the caliper from the disc, tying it to a convenient point to prevent it hanging by the attached hydraulic pipe. Note the number of shims fitted between the caliper and vertical link.

To remove the hub grease cap, screw a No. 10 A.F. setscrew provided in the tool kit into the tapped hole in the grease cap, or prise off the cap, exposing the hub retaining nut. Remove the split-pin, retaining nut, washer and outer bearing. The hub assembly and inner bearing can then

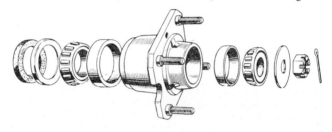

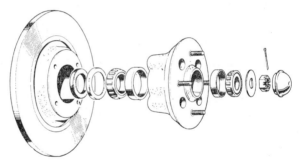

FIG. 12. FRONT WHEEL HUBS DISMANTLED

Above, hub used with drum brakes.
Below, hub fitted to disc-braked cars.

be drawn off. A gentle rocking movement should be applied to the hub in order to free it.

The old grease should be wiped away with a piece of clean rag that is free from fluff. The hub and bearings should be washed in clean paraffin, taking care to lay the parts out on a clean rag or on a sheet of paper on the bench in order to avoid the slightest risk of picking up any grit, which is fatal to any form of ball or roller bearing. The hub should be packed with a good-quality general-purpose grease and replaced on the front axle, followed by reassembly of the parts in the reverse order to dismantling. If there has been any sign of leakage of grease from the hub, remove the old felt seal, thoroughly clean the retainer and cement a new seal in place with jointing compound.

The nut should be tightened up until a perceptible drag can be felt at the wheel. The nut should then be slackened back until the wheel is just free to rotate, with just perceptible end-float. This may best be checked by attempting to rock the outside of the wheel by hand. It should just be possible to detect very slight play. The official figure quoted is 0·002–0·008 in. end-float on the bearing.

It should be emphasized that this adjustment is a critical one and that the wheel should be rotated during the whole of the adjusting process. Too tight an adjustment will cause rapid wear of the bearings; too loose an adjustment will also cause bearing wear and may adversely affect the steering. If in doubt, therefore, it is better to leave the work to a Standard-Triumph dealer.

When the correct adjustment has been obtained a new split-pin should be fitted and the ends correctly bent back. The grease cap should be packed with fresh grease before it is replaced. After refitting the wheel, check the tightness of the wheel nuts when the wheel has been lowered to the ground. Then refit the hub cap and repeat the operation on the other front wheel.

Greasing Steering Gearbox. Turn the steering to full left lock for right-hand-drive cars and to right lock for left-hand-drive models. Unscrew the plug from the box, fit a nipple and give five strokes of the gun only, using general-purpose grease. Over-greasing may damage the rubber bellows. Leave the nipple in place or remove it and refit the plug, as preferred.

Dynamo Lubrication. The front bearing on the dynamo or generator is packed with lubricant on assembly and should require no attention in the ordinary way. Only the rear bearing requires lubrication and this should be done by applying a few drops of oil through the hole in the centre of the endplate boss. If this bearing is over-lubricated, the excess of oil may find its way on to the commutator, causing a reduction in the charging rate, or complete loss of charge.

Descaling and Flushing Cooling System. At least once a year—preferably in the autumn and in the spring if an anti-freezing compound is used—the system should be drained, flushed-out and refilled. If the water does not flow freely from the radiator drain tap and from the tap on the side of the engine cylinder block, the openings should be probed with a piece of wire to dislodge any accumulated sediment—or better still, unscrew and remove the taps. A hose should then be inserted in the filler neck and water allowed to flow through the system until clean water issues from the taps.

Before flushing the system it is an advantage to run the car for a day or two with a proprietary non-corrosive compound added to the cooling water. These compounds will remove any deposits of rust or scale which might be sealing minor leaks. If anti-freezing compound is used without descaling the system, there is a risk that its very "searching" action may find such weak spots, with possibly serious consequences if a leak should develop and continue undetected during the course of a lengthy run.

If an interior heater is fitted and the cooling system has been drained, make sure that the heater water-control tap is open when refilling the

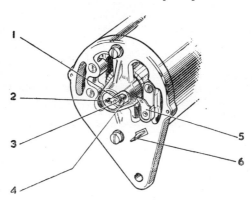

FIG. 13. DYNAMO END-BEARING LUBRICATION

1. Felt ring retainer
2 Inject oil here
3. Felt ring
4. Porous bronze bush
5. Output terminal "D"
6. Field terminal "F"

radiator. It is a good plan to slacken the clamp on the upper heater hose when the heater is fitted on the engine bulkhead, or the clamp at the radiator end of the hose when a recirculatory type of heater is fitted, and to loosen the hose in order to dispel any air-lock that may develop in the heater. Do not tighten the clamp until water is flowing from this point and re-check the level in the header tank after the engine has been running for a few minutes.

Curing Leaks. Proprietary chemical anti-leak compounds are usually quite effective in curing small leakages. One sometimes sees the use of such substances as flour, porridge or mustard recommended: but while these may sometimes be effective and must be used in a real emergency, the very serious risk of blocking the small passages in the radiator, necessitating the fitting of a new radiator film block, cannot be overlooked.

A further point is that even a first-class proprietary anti-leak compound will not be effective if it builds-up on top of deposits of scale or rust; the most satisfactory course, therefore, is thoroughly to flush-out and descale the system, as previously described, before using one of these compounds.

The Thermostat. Although the thermostat which regulates the cooling water temperature vitally affects engine efficiency it is often overlooked and seldom checked. It consists of a valve, operated by a bellows or by a wax-filled capsule, fitted at the water outlet from the cylinder head, that

Fig. 14. REMOVING THE THERMOSTAT

prevents circulation of water to the radiator until the normal running temperature is reached.

With either type of thermostat a "winter" version, which opens at a higher temperature, can be obtained. This shortens the warming-up period in cold weather and improves the efficiency of the heater. Strictly speaking, the standard thermostat should be refitted in the Spring, but this is seldom necessary in temperate climates.

Thermostats, of course, are not infallible and if overheating occurs, or conversely if the engine is slow to warm-up, it is logical to check this item. Remember, however, that overheating can be caused by a number of other faults, among which deposits of rust and lime scale in the cylinder head and radiator water passages are the most likely: shortage of oil or water, obstructed air passages in the radiator, over-retarded ignition and severe pinking will also cause the trouble.

The thermostat can be lifted out after the water outlet elbow has been removed. When cold the valve should be tightly closed. If it is open, either the bellows is punctured or the stem is jammed by an accumulation of lime deposits.

If the thermostat appears to be serviceable, it should be tested by immersing it in a pan of water which should be brought nearly up to boiling point. If a suitable thermometer is available the opening temperature should be checked while moving the thermostat about in the water to ensure even heating; the temperature will, of course, depend on the type of thermostat fitted, as described above. If the valve has not opened when the water begins to boil a replacement thermostat should be fitted. Before refitting a used thermostat make sure that the small air-release hole in the valve is not choked; otherwise an air-lock is likely to occur when the cooling system is refilled.

Crankcase Breather Valve. Some engines are fitted with a crankcase breather valve which regulates the flow of fume-laden air from the rocker cover into the inlet manifold. If this valve does not operate properly, it may be impossible to obtain satisfactory idling in spite of adjustment resulting in the formation of deposits of oil sludge. It is a simple matter to dismantle the valve by disengaging the clip and lifting out the top cover diaphragm and spring. Clean the parts in methylated spirits and make sure that the breather pipe is not blocked.

Whenever you clean the valve, take off the oil filler cap and make sure that the breather hole is unobstructed and that the sealing washer is in good condition.

2 Decarbonizing and Engine Overhaul

In pre-war instruction manuals and motorists' handbooks a good deal of space used to be devoted to the subject of decarbonizing and "top-overhauls." In the "thirties" for example it was not unusual for a manufacturer to recommend that the cylinder head should be removed at intervals of say, 5,000 or 7,000 miles, to allow carbon deposits to be cleaned from the combustion chambers and piston crowns—and that during every second decarbonization it might be a good plan to remove the valves for examination and grinding-in to restore a gas-tight seal.

Nowadays, however, the subject is seldom dealt with in manufacturers' handbooks, the usual recommendation being that this work should be left to an appointed dealer or agent. Admittedly there is some justification for this change of heart on the part of most manufacturers; by pre-war standards modern engine oils and fuels deposit only negligible amounts of carbon in the combustion chambers: on a modern small, highly-stressed engine, it is the valves that have become the determining factor-particularly the exhaust valves, which often need refacing or replacement after a life of about 15,000–20,000 miles. This work can be done most efficiently by using special valve and valve-seating reconditioning equipment. This does not mean, however, that a practical owner can no longer tackle the work himself; the engine could hardly be more accessible and if the sequence described in this chapter is followed and each step carried out conscientiously, first-class results should be obtained. Where expert assistance is required, it is a simple matter to take the parts to the local Standard-Triumph dealer for reconditioning.

When is a Top-overhaul Needed? It is a sound recommendation that an engine that is running well should not be disturbed: on the other hand if decarbonizing and attention to the valves is postponed for too long, the amount of work involved, and the expense incurred, may be greater than would have been the case had the head been removed at an earlier stage. Badly burnt exhaust valves, for example, must be scrapped, whereas slightly pitted valves can be given another lease of life by refacing and grinding-in.

Moreover, an engine that has a relatively high compression ratio, will benefit from the removal of even a light coating of carbon which retards the flow of heat through the piston crowns to the lubricating oil, which acts as a coolant as well as a lubricant. Overheating that results from carbon deposits is probably more directly responsible for causing detonation or "pinking" than the slight increase in compression ratio caused by the deposit itself.

The exhaust valves can also cause pinking when they become overheated. Most of the heat from the head of the valve is transferred through the seating to the cooling water during the instant that the valve is closed; it is not surprising, therefore, that restoring a good contact between the valve and seating by careful grinding-in will often cure an acute case of pinking.

The need for a top-overhaul will be indicated by a progressive deterioration in performance, sometimes accompanied by a tendency of the engine to overheat and for "pinking" to occur at low speeds in top gear, together with symptoms of pre-ignition and a tendency for the engine to run-on when the ignition is switched off.

It is possible to delay the point at which decarbonization is necessary by slightly retarding the ignition, as described in Chapter 3, but this should be regarded as a purely temporary measure as the valves will probably require attention.

Engine Tests. Most service stations can check the compression of each cylinder with the aid of a special pressure gauge. The compression should be equal on all cylinders and each cylinder should show a distinct, springy "bounce" as top-dead-centre is reached and passed. If the compression is weak on one or more cylinders the most likely cause is burnt or pitted valve faces. Leakage of gases past the piston rings cannot, of course, be discounted, but this fault will normally be accompanied by excessive oil consumption.

Apart from the compression test, a reliable indication of the general condition of the engine can be obtained by the use of a manifold vacuum gauge of the type that is included, for example, in the Redex Do-it-yourself Tuning Kit, following the detailed instructions for engine testing that are supplied with the particular kit. A practical owner will quickly find such a gauge invaluable, not only in diagnosing such faults as burnt or sticking valves, worn piston rings and defective sparking plugs, but also in carrying out carburettor and ignition timing adjustments.

Tools and Spares Required. Before starting work it is necessary to assemble, in addition to the usual tools used for routine maintenance, a valve-spring compressor (it may be possible to hire this from a local garage, as it will not be required again until the engine is next decarbonized), a blunt scraper, a valve-grinding tool of the rubber suction-cup type, a small tin of valve-grinding paste containing both fine and coarse grades, a plentiful supply of clean rags, free from fluff, a selection of boxes, tins or jars in which small parts can be deposited, pending reassembly, a wire brush, paraffin and a dish or tray in which to swill the parts.

It is advisable to renew all gaskets, not forgetting the water-pump joint washer. The expense is small and is an insurance against water or gas leakages after the engine has been reassembled, which would, of course, entail the dismantling and reassembly of the parts. If a defective cylinder-head gasket allows water to leak into the cylinders, serious damage may be done. Again, although no external leakage may be apparent, gas may leak between adjacent cylinders, where the gasket is narrow and is subject to relatively high pressure, causing misfiring and loss of power which may be difficult to diagnose.

A set of new valve springs is a worthwhile investment. If the top-overhaul is carried out properly it can be anticipated that the car will run for upwards of 20,000 miles before the head is next removed; but "tired" valve springs can undo all the careful work into the overhaul.

When purchasing these parts, ask the dealer whether he can let you have an old piston ring which will fit the bores; this will be useful when decarbonizing the pistons, as described later.

Removing the Cylinder Head. Drain the cooling system and disconnect the battery cable at both of the terminal posts in order to prevent the possibility of any "shorts." Disconnect the sparking plug leads and number each cable to avoid confusion on reassembly. At this stage it is advisable to remove the sparking plugs, putting them aside for cleaning and resetting of the gaps. If an engine temperature gauge is fitted, detach the wire from the transmitter on the water-hose elbow.

Remove the air cleaner and disconnect the carburettor controls, the petrol pipe and the vacuum pipe to the distributor. The carburettor or carburettors may now be removed or may, if preferred, be left in place and removed later with the manifolds. On single-carburettor models, remove the manifold drain pipe.

Slacken the securing clips and remove the radiator hose and heater connexions, if fitted. Take off the water-pipe elbow and remove the thermostat.

Remove the nuts securing the exhaust pipe clamp to the exhaust manifold. The manifold securing nuts can now be removed and the manifolds taken off. Alternatively they can be removed later, when the cylinder head is on the bench; this is probably more convenient.

Attention should next be turned to the valve rocker shaft assembly. Remove the rocker cover from the top of the cylinder head and unscrew the nuts that retain the rocker shaft brackets; the rocker assembly can then be lifted off.

The eight push-rods that operate the rockers should next be with-drawn, one at a time, and laid out in order in a place where they are not likely to be disturbed, so that they can be refitted in their original positions when the engine is reassembled; this is important, as in service the ball-ends and cups on the rods become lapped to the tappets and rocker screws with which they mate.

Slacken the dynamo pivot bolts and disconnect the adjusting link. allowing the dynamo to be swung inwards and the fan belt removed. The water pump and fan can then be unbolted and removed as an assembly.

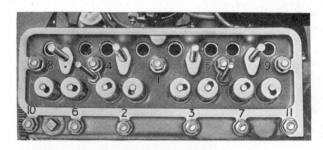

FIG. 15. CORRECT SEQUENCE FOR TIGHTENING OR SLACKENING
CYLINDER-HEAD NUTS
Above: Four-cylinder engines. *Below:* Six-cylinder engines

The cylinder head is now ready to be lifted off the cylinder block. Unscrew the nuts progressively in the sequence shown in Fig. 15.

If the head does not come away easily, no attempt should be made to prise it up by inserting a screwdriver or similar tool between the head and the block, as this may damage the machined surfaces. A sharp tap with a wooden mallet, or with a hammer on a block of wood held against the side of the head, should free the joint.

Remove the manifolds and carburettor or carburettors and put the various parts aside for later attention.

Decarbonizing the Pistons. Rotate the crankshaft with the starting handle until two of the pistons are at the tops of the cylinders. Stuff clean rags into the bores of the remaining two cylinders and in the push-rod openings, the water-ways and the oil-feed drilling in the cylinder head.

Remove the carbon from the piston crowns with a suitable blunt scraper, taking care not to score the surfaces. Then burnish the crowns with a wire brush. Do not use an abrasive, such as metal polish, owing

FIG. 16. DECARBONIZING A PISTON

1. Clean-out water-transfer holes. 2. Leave ring of carbon around piston crown.
3. Use blunt scraper

to the risk of particles being trapped in the piston ring grooves or between the rings and the cylinder walls.

Most authorities recommend that a narrow ring of carbon should be left around the edge of the piston crown and that the ring around the edge of the cylinder bore should not be disturbed as these can form a useful oil seal if the piston rings and bores are no longer in perfect condition. This is where an old piston ring comes into the picture: placed on top of the piston, it provides a mask to protect the carbon seal from the scraper and the wire brush.

Decarbonizing the Cylinder Head and Valves. It is best to decarbonize the combustion chambers before removing the valves, as there will then be no risk of damaging the valve seatings. Every trace of carbon should be scraped off and the surfaces should then be burnished with a wire brush; a cup-shaped brush, used in the chuck of an electric drill, is ideal for this job but patient hand work will give equally good results.

The mating faces of the head should also be cleaned, taking particular care not to score them. The valves can then be removed. The best tool to use to compress the valve springs is the official service compressor but if this is not available a piece of wood should be shaped to fit a combustion chamber and the head should be placed over this on the bench, so that the heads of the valves rest against the wood.

On single-carburettor engines the springs are retained by caps which must be pressed downward and then moved sideways to disengage them

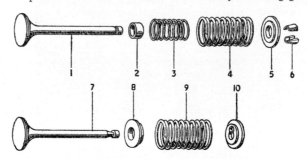

FIG. 17. VALVE-SPRING AND VALVE ASSEMBLIES

Vitesse, Spitfire and twin-carburettor
948 c.c. engines (*upper*)

1. Valve
2. Collar
3. Inner spring (Vitesse only)
4. Outer spring
5. Collar (in two parts on Vitesse exhaust valves)

Single-carburettor 948 c.c., 1200 and
12/50 Herald engines (*lower*)

6. Split cone cotters
7. Valve
8. Collar
9. Spring
10. Collar

from the ends of the valve stems. On twin-carburettor cylinder heads, double valve springs are used; the spring caps are retained by split-cone cotters, which are more easily removed if a valve-spring compressor is used to compress the springs.

Discard the valve springs if, as recommended earlier, a new set is to be fitted. Otherwise stand them in line on a level surface and discard any that are noticeably shorter than the others or which have distorted coils.

As each valve is withdrawn from its guide it should be placed in the correct order on the bench. The valves should not be interchanged. It is a good plan to drill holes in a length of wood or in a strip of cardboard to take the stems and to number these to correspond with the positions in the head.

The undersides of the valve heads, the stems and the ports in the head, which could not be reached when the valves were in position, should now be thoroughly cleaned. Care must be taken not to score the seatings on the valves and in the combustion chambers.

The valve stems should be scraped clean. Emery cloth should not be used on the sections that work in the guides. The guides themselves should be cleaned out by drawing a paraffin-soaked rag through them. Each valve should then be checked for fit in its own guide. Any noticeable degree of sideways shake indicates the need for new valves and guides; the best plan is to take the head to a Standard dealer for advice and, if he confirms the diagnosis, to allow him to fit the new guides and recut

FIG. 18. BADLY-PITTED VALVES SHOULD BE REFACED IN A SPECIAL MACHINE

the seatings with special equipment. It is useless to grind-in the valves when the stems and guides are worn, or to fit new guides without recutting the seatings in the head.

Similarly, if the seatings on the valves and in the cylinder head are badly pitted, they must be recut with special abrasive stones and the valve faces trued up in a suitable machine. Excessive grinding-in, in an attempt to remove deep pitting, results in recessed seatings and incorrect mating angles which cause loss of power. It is then necessary to cut the seatings first with a 15-degree cutter, to narrow them, followed by the normal 45-degree cutter.

Grinding-in the Valves. If the valves and seatings are in good condition, or have received the appropriate treatment as described above, the next step is to grind-in—or, more correctly, lap-in—each valve on to its seating in order to obtain a gas-tight seal.

Valve-grinding paste is usually supplied in two grades, fine and coarse, in one container. The coarse grade should be used only in an emergency, to remove deep pitting when proper reconditioning cannot be carried out, but light pitting may be removed with the fine paste until a good matt finish has been obtained.

FIG. 19. CORRECT METHOD OF HOLDING SUCTION-CUP TOOL WHEN GRINDING-IN VALVES

Each valve should be rotated quickly and lightly with the suction-cup grinding tool, first in one direction and then in the other, spinning the handle of the tool between the palms of the hands as shown in Fig. 19. From time to time the valve should be raised from its seat and turned a quarter of a turn, grinding being continued from this new position. This will ensure that an even, concentric surface is obtained. Only a light downward pressure on the valve is required.

When correctly ground, both the valve seat and the face of the valve should have an even, clean, grey matt finish with no signs of bright rings or any evidence of pitting. Bright rings are caused by grinding with insufficient grinding paste, while "tramlines" are usually the result of continuously grinding the valve on its seat without taking up a different position.

A useful test to check the effectiveness of the seal is to make a series of pencil marks across the seating face of the valve with a soft lead pencil. Replace the valve and rotate it once through a quarter of a turn on its seating. If the valve is seating properly, each pencil mark should be erased at the line of contact. If some of the lines are not broken, the indication is that either the valve or its seating is not truly circular and that renewal or refacing of the valve or seat (or both) is required.

When all the valves have been ground-in the valves and seatings should be thoroughly cleaned and all traces of grinding paste removed with a piece of clean cloth and a little petrol. Lubricate the valve stems with a little clean engine oil before refitting the valves in their correct positions and reassembling the springs and retainers. Make sure that the valve spring cap or each pair of cotters, as the case may be, is correctly seated on the valve stem.

Oil Leakage from Push-rod Tubes. If there are signs of oil leakage at the joints between the push-rod tubes and the cylinder head, the head should be taken to a Standard-Triumph dealer, who will have a special tool which is used to swage the ends of the tubes into the countersunk recesses in the cylinder head, thus restoring oil-tight joints.

Replacing the Cylinder Head. Before refitting the cylinder head make sure that the piston crowns, cylinder walls and the top of the block are scrupulously clean. Pour a small quantity of engine oil around each bore so that it will be distributed over the cylinder walls and down the sides of the pistons when the engine is first turned over.

The new cylinder-head gasket should be smeared on both faces with high-melting-point grease and eased down over the studs. Never use gasket cement, as this is likely to cause subsequent leakage. The copper-asbestos gasket fitted to single-carburettor engines should have the seamed face downwards, whereas the steel gasket used on twin-carburettor heads should be fitted with the swaged sealing faces upwards. The cylinder head retaining nuts should be progressively tightened in the sequence shown in Fig. 15.

Place the eight push-rods in position, making sure that they locate in their respective tappets, and place the rocker shaft assembly on the studs. Carefully work it into position, making sure that the rocker adjusting screws engage properly in the push-rod cups. Tighten the nuts down evenly.

Adjust the valve clearances as described on page 14. The remainder of the reassembly is quite straightforward. Make sure that the petrol drain pipe fitted to single-carburettor manifolds and the passage in the inlet manifold leading to it are clear. Use a new joint washer when refitting the water pump and coat both sides with sealing compound.

After a final check all round, refill the cooling system and start the engine.

If a heater is fitted, check the level of the water in the header tank after the engine has been running for a few minutes. When the engine

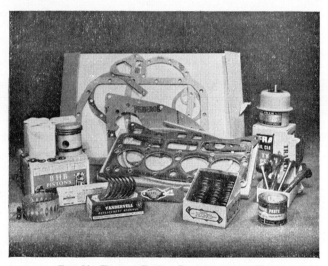

Fig. 20. Typical Engine Reconditioning Kit

is well warmed-up, switch off and go over the cylinder-head and manifold nuts again. The nuts should be checked a second time after about 300 miles' running. Remember to readjust the valve clearances on each occasion, as they will be reduced when the cylinder head is pulled down.

When the engine has been decarbonized, the ignition timing should be checked as described in Chapter 3. It is usually possible to advance the ignition slightly. Also, the carburettor slow-running mixture strength and speed will usually require readjustment, as described in Chapter 4.

MAJOR OVERHAULS

If the engine has covered a very high mileage a partial overhaul may not be very effective. It will probably be necessary to rebore the cylinders and fit oversize pistons, regrind the crankshaft journals to take undersize connecting-rod and main bearing shells and renew the timing chain and sprockets and possibly also the oil pump and the starter ring gear. Undoubtedly the most satisfactory course in such cases will be to install a new engine under the service-exchange scheme.

It is surprising how often, however, that an owner is persuaded to have a new engine fitted when, in fact, heavy oil consumption, piston slap and low oil pressure could be cured by an expenditure of quite a small sum— seldom exceeding £5–£10—provided that the owner is prepared to carry out the necessary dismantling and assembly and to send the worn components to a specialist firm for reconditioning or replacement. If the engine has not covered more than about 30,000 miles, careful consideration should be given to this project.

A New Lease of Life for Your Engine. One firm that has made a special study of the effectiveness of reconditioning small modern engines in this manner is G.M.A. Reconsets Ltd., 119 Uxbridge Road, London, W.12. As a result of their experience, they supply a standard reconditioning kit which includes new pistons, fitted with special oil-control rings (normally rendering reboring unnecessary), a set of connecting-rod bearing shells, new exhaust valves, and a complete set of valve springs, a timing chain, a complete set of gaskets, gasket cement and graphite assembly compound. Even a piston-ring clamp is included.

If a workshop manual is not available for reference, a Service Data Sheet can be added to the kit at the cost of a couple of shillings or so.

In deciding whether a partial overhaul will be satisfactory, the condition of the crankshaft is likely to be more important than the amount of wear in the cylinder bores. Excessive connecting-rod bearing clearances can result in more oil reaching the bores than can be controlled even by new pistons and special oil-control rings. If the engine has covered more than 40,000 miles, therefore, it would be as well to enlist the aid of someone who can measure the crankpins with a micrometer. If the wear exceeds 0·001 in., it is advisable to have the crankshaft re-ground. Even half a "thou" of wear can cause an appreciable increase in oil consumption.

Fortunately, fitting new connecting-rod bearing shells is usually all that is required when a partial overhaul is undertaken at between 20,000–30,000 miles. In any event, the shells should be replaced as a matter of routine at this mileage. It is a very straightforward job as the bearings are of the thin-shell type which can be installed without the need for skilled fitting. No shims are used and the caps should on no account be filed or rubbed down to take up excessive clearance. Provided that the crankpins are not scored or badly worn, the installation of new bearing shells will give the correct running clearance and restore normal oil pressure.

It is estimated that an engine which is reconditioned to this extent after having covered about 30,000 miles can be run to a total life of 60,000 miles before a complete overhaul is required. Obviously, an overhaul of this type is a worthwhile proposition—particularly if the ignition distributor and the carburettor are replaced by reconditioned components under the service-exchange scheme. It is false economy to refit worn auxiliaries to an overhauled engine.

It must be assumed, of course, that an owner who is prepared to tackle this type of work will have had some experience of engine dismantling, fitting and assembly or will be able to rely on the guidance of an experienced mechanic. Alternatively the do-it-yourself owner can avoid most of the pitfalls by referring to a practical handbook, such as *Engine Repair for the Owner-Driver* and *Automobile Workshop Practice*, which are published in the Pitman Automobile Maintenance Series.

3 Servicing the Ignition System

IF the ignition system is to continue to function efficiently for many thousands of miles, it requires a little more attention than the routine maintenance described in Chapter 1, supplemented, perhaps, by an occasional cursory examination of the sparking plug leads and low-tension wiring.

For example, an owner will often go to the expense of fitting a new set of sparking plugs, resulting in only a moderate improvement in the running, whereas renewal of the relatively inexpensive contact-breaker points would have transformed the performance of the engine. Unfortunately, instruction books seldom emphasize the benefit of renewing these vital contacts whenever a new set of sparking plugs is fitted—say at 10,000–15,000-mile intervals.

At the same time it is also an advantage to have the distributor tested by a garage or an auto-electrical specialist who possesses a motorized test-panel on which the distributor can be checked while being driven at various speeds. Only with equipment of this type is it possible to diagnose faults such as weak centrifugal timing control springs, worn advance mechanism and incorrect or erratic action of the vacuum timing control. A distributor should certainly be tested—or replaced under the service-exchange scheme—when the engine is decarbonized or overhauled. Otherwise one cannot expect to obtain the full benefit from the work put into the engine.

In this chapter it is proposed to deal with the finer points of ignition system servicing which are often overlooked, but which call for no specialized electrical knowledge or equipment.

THE SPARKING PLUGS

The sparking plugs face arduous working conditions, being subject to extremes of heat and to the formation of carbon deposits. On older cars, in which an increased amount of oil reaches the combustion chambers as the result of piston-ring, cylinder and valve-guide wear, it is usually necessary to clean the plugs at fairly frequent intervals if poor performance, unsatisfactory fuel consumption and difficult starting are to be avoided. It seems logical, therefore, to deal first with these very important items and then work back through the other components in the ignition system.

Sparking plug efficiency depends on three rules: fit the correct grade of plugs; service them at regular intervals—at least every 6,000 miles, and more frequently if the engine is no longer in first-class condition—and renew them while they still have a reasonable remaining lease of life. Keeping plugs in use until they are completely worn out is an expensive form of economy.

When plug trouble does develop, try to arrive at the basic cause before blaming the plugs themselves. Retarded ignition timing, overheating, excessive oil consumption or a weak carburettor mixture are some of the factors that can affect plug performance.

Choosing the Correct Plug. An engine manufacturer must necessarily choose a type of plug which is suitable for the "normal" or average service

FIG. 21. CHOOSING A SUITABLE PLUG

Left: This plug is running too cold; it shows obvious signs of oiling up. *Centre*: The light deposits on this plug indicate normal heat conditions. *Right*: The "bleached" appearance and lack of deposits on this plug are signs of overheating.

that a particular vehicle is likely to encounter under average conditions but this does not mean that the recommended grade will be suitable in every case.

For example, the owner who indulges in continuous high-speed driving may find that the normal grade of plug has a tendency to overheat, causing pinking, misfiring at high speed and rapid burning of the electrodes. The same may apply, to a lesser degree, if long spells of driving in low gear are indulged in when climbing mountain passes. A "cooler" grade of plug which is able to withstand the greater amount of heat developed under these conditions is the obvious answer—possibly a "sports" plug if the engine has been modified or if a tuning kit has been fitted.

Much "local" driving, on the other hand, entailing frequent stopping and starting and comparatively long periods of running during which the engine does not become fully warmed-up, may cause excessive carbon deposits on the plug insulators, indicating the need for a "hotter" grade of plug which will burn off these deposits. This also applies if the engine is worn and an excessive amount of oil is reaching the combustion chambers. A "hotter" plug can also be fitted when high-octane fuels are used.

The recommended grades of plug are given in Chapter 7. These are suitable for normal running conditions. If a "hotter" plug, which will burn off excessive oil or carbon deposits, is needed, or a "colder" grade to resist overheating or pre-ignition, the appropriate alternatives will be found in the plug manufacturers' heat-range charts that can be consulted at most garages. If in doubt, have a word with your Triumph dealer.

Cleaning and Inspecting Sparking Plugs. The plug spanner must be handled carefully to avoid cracking the insulator. Make sure that it fits securely over the plug. After unscrewing the plugs see that the sealing washers do not fall off and become lost.

The most effective method of removing the carbon deposits is the use of a plug-cleaning machine in which a high-pressure air blast carries a fine abrasive into the interior of the plug, thoroughly scouring the insulator, the inner walls and points.

When it is not possible to have the plugs cleaned at a service station the work can be done quite efficiently at home with the aid of the Techniblaster plug cleaner, which operates on the same principle as the garage plug cleaner but in which the air pressure is obtained by connecting the cleaner to a tyre pump. Oily plugs should first be swilled out with petrol. About half a dozen strokes of the pump will clean the plug and the rubber connector can be disconnected from the cleaner and used to blow out any remaining abrasive from the plug. Grains that are trapped between the insulator and the interior of the plug can be dislodged with a stout darning needle or a short length of wire, hammered flat at one end. In passing it may be mentioned that some garage mechanics overlook this very important point.

A useful tip known to plug specialists is to true-up the sides of the electrodes lightly with a small, fine-cut file, to restore the sharp corners that existed when the plug was new. This will considerably reduce the voltage needed to produce a spark across the gap.

The threaded portion of each plug should be cleaned with a stiff wire brush and a smear of graphite grease placed on the threads. This will ensure that the plug will tighten down easily and will facilitate removal when the next cleaning and adjustment is due. Make sure that the sealing washers are in good condition and tighten the plugs, using hand pressure only on the tommy-bar to ensure a gas-tight joint. Too much force should never be used and is unnecessary.

The dynamo obstructs access to No. 1 plug to some extent. To avoid any risk of cross-threading the plug when replacing it, it is best to screw it in by hand, reserving the plug spanner for the last half-turn or so.

Changing to a different type of fan belt may make the plug more accessible, as mentioned on page 17.

Adjusting the Plug Gaps. After the plugs have been cleaned and the points trued-up as just described, the gap should be adjusted by bending the side electrode *only*. One of the inexpensive combination gauges and setting tools sold by plug manufacturers is a worthwhile investment. If

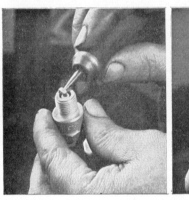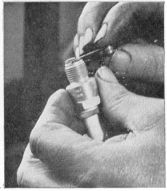

FIG. 22. SETTING PLUG GAPS

When levering-up the side electrode (*left*), avoid applying pressure to the central wire. Keep the feeler gauge square with the electrodes when checking the gap.

an improvised method is used (Fig. 22) make sure that no leverage is exerted against the central electrode; otherwise the internal insulator will probably be cracked, rendering the plug useless.

The recommended gap of 0·025 in. (25 thousandths) will give best results under all normal conditions. If the plugs are prone to oil-up, a smaller gap may be tried—say, 0·020 or 0·022 in.—but this must be regarded as a palliative rather than a cure. If the prospect of an engine overhaul is rather remote, the use of a spark intensifier, as described on page 50, will usually enable the normal gap to be restored without the risk of misfiring or difficult starting.

THE DISTRIBUTOR

Working back through the ignition system we come to the distributor, which not only distributes the high-tension current to the sparking plugs but also includes a contact-breaker that interrupts the low-voltage current passing from the battery through the ignition coil (as described in more

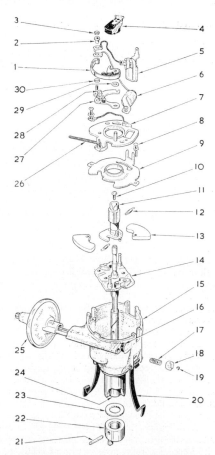

FIG. 23. LUCAS IGNITION DISTRIBUTOR

A Delco-Remy distributor is shown in Fig. 32.

1. Spring contact
2. Insulating sleeve
3. Nut
4. Rotor arm
5. Low-tension terminal
6. Capacitor (condenser)
7 Contact plate
8. Screw
9. Baseplate
10. Screw
11. Cam
12. Centrifugal spring
13. Centrifugal weights
14. Action plate and shaft assembly
15. Distributor body

16. Ratchet spring
17. Coiled spring
18. Adjusting nut
19. Circlip
20. Cap retainer
21. Pin
22. Driving dog
23. Washer
24. Bearing sleeve
25. Vacuum unit
26. Vacuum connecting spring
27. Fixed contact
28. Screw
29. Insulating washer
30. Insulating washer

detail later), and automatic timing devices that vary the timing of the sparks at the plugs to suit the engine running conditions, speed and throttle opening at any moment.

Lucas distributors are fitted to Herald, Courier and early Vitesse engines. Later Vitesse and the Spitfire engines have Delco-Remy equipment (*see* Fig. 27).

Servicing the Contact-breaker Points. Most instruction manuals dismiss the all-important subject of contact-breaker maintenance far too briefly. It cannot be too strongly emphasized, for example, that the gap between the contact-breaker points should never be measured with a feeler gauge unless the points have previously been trued-up with a fine carborundum stone or with very fine emery cloth. After only a few hundred miles of running a small "pip" forms on one point and a corresponding "crater" on the other, owing to the transference of microscopic particles of metal by the spark that occurs whenever the points open. The "pip" renders it impossible to obtain a correct reading with a feeler gauge.

The correct gap between the points is 0·015 in. A 0·014 in. feeler gauge should slide in fairly easily, while a 0·016 in. blade should be a fairly tight fit. To achieve this degree of accuracy the points must obviously be in a good condition.

Remove the distributor cap by springing aside the two retaining clips. To render the contact-breaker points more accessible, pull off the rotor. If it is a tight fit, gentle leverage can be applied with the tip of a screwdriver, taking care not to crack the plastic. It will be seen that a projection on the interior surface of the rotor fits into a slot in the distributor shaft so that replacement is possible only in one position.

The contact-breaker points should now be separated with the finger. The faces should have a clean, frosted appearance, apart from the development of the small pip and crater.

The spring to which the movable contact arm is attached is retained by the nut on the terminal post. On all distributors except that fitted to the Spitfire and Vitesse, the arm can be pulled off its pivot when this nut has been removed. Make a careful note of the positions of the insulating washers and sleeve. The fixed contact plate can then be taken out, after removing the screw that retains it.

On the Spitfire and Vitesse distributors, take out the screw that clamps the fixed contact plate and lift the contact-breaker assembly sufficiently to allow the nut on the terminal post which retains the two terminal tags and the fixed end of the contact-breaker spring to be unscrewed. Remove the capacitor and lift the contacts out of the distributor.

If the contact points are badly burnt the safest plan is to renew them, as It is difficult to keep the surfaces square if it is necessary to remove a fair amount of metal with a carborundum stone.

Adjusting Contact-breaker Gap. When the contact-breaker points have been trued and reassembled correctly (not forgetting the fibre insulating washer beneath the moving arm) the gap should be adjusted. The projection on the fibre block must be exactly on the crest of one of the "humps" of the cam. A slight movement of the cam in either direction will give a false reading. When a starting handle is not fitted, the best plan is to remove the sparking plugs and ease the engine round by pulling on the fan belt.

To adjust the gap, slacken the screw that retains the fixed contact plate. On Lucas distributors insert the blade of a screwdriver in a notch in the edge of the plate and turn it clockwise to reduce the gap or anti-clockwise to increase it. On some Delco-Remy distributors fitted to Spitfire and Vitesse engines, there is an eccentric adjusting screw in an elongated hole next to the locking screw. By turning this (after slackening the locking screw) the gap between the contacts can be adjusted. On later Vitesse distributors the eccentric adjuster is not fitted and the fixed contact plate must be moved with the tip of a screwdriver.

The Ignition Condenser. If the contact-breaker points are badly burned the trouble may be due to too small a gap, which will seriously reduce the life of the points. In most cases, however, it is logical to suspect the condenser, which is connected across the contact points in order to absorb the surge of current that builds up in the primary winding of the ignition coil (in addition to the current induced in the high-tension winding), and which, in the absence of a condenser, would cause a destructive arc across the contact-breaker points, instead of the normal slight spark. The condenser also discharges back through the primary windings, causing a more rapid collapse of the magnetic flux and a more intense spark at the sparking plug. It will be obvious, therefore, that an inefficient condenser will not only cause rapid burning of the points but will also result in a weak spark or—if it should short-circuit internally—failure of the plugs to fire at all.

When misfiring and difficult starting are experienced the best test is to substitute a new condenser, or one that is known to be sound. Before finally condemning a condenser make sure that there is no break or short-circuit in the flexible lead connecting it to the contact-breaker terminal post and that the condenser is efficiently "earthed."

Distributor Rotor and Cap. The high-tension current from the coil enters the centre of the distributor cap and passes to the rotor through a spring-loaded brush—actually, a short pencil-shaped length of carbon which also acts as a suppressor to reduce the interference that would otherwise be picked up by nearby radio and television receivers. From the brass tip of the rotor the current jumps in turn to each of the terminals in the distributor cap, to which the sparking plug leads are connected in sequence to give the correct firing order 1, 3, 4, 2 for four-cylinder engines and 1, 5, 3, 6, 2, 4 for six-cylinder units.

The brass contact on the rotor and the terminals inside the cap should be scraped bright and clean. The carbon brush should also be checked.

FIG. 24. SERVICING POINTS ON THE IGNITION DISTRIBUTOR
(*See also* Fig. 8)

1. Electrode connected to plug lead
2. Central spring-loaded electrode
3. Distributor cap
4. Vacuum timing control
5. Nut securing contact spring
6. Low-tension terminal
   (condenser in background)
7. Rotor

It does not wear away quickly but sometimes tends to stick in its guide. Do not overstretch the spring and be careful not to break the brush.

Any accumulation of dust or oily deposits inside the cap, which will tend to attract moisture in damp weather and thus provide a leakage path for the high-tension current, should be removed with petrol and the interior surface polished with a clean cloth. If current has been leaking between the terminals, it will have left evidence in the form of dark tracks on the surface of the plastic. Sometimes these can be removed by a thorough cleaning with metal polish but bad "tracking" usually calls for renewal of the cap.

Similarly, the rotor should be thoroughly examined for signs of tracking. Occasionally internal leakage develops from the underside of the brass electrode through the plastic to the interior surface, allowing the high-tension current to jump to the cam spindle and so to earth. Needless to

FIG. 25. CORRECT CONNECTIONS FOR SPARKING PLUG LEADS

say, this can be a very elusive fault to spot unless one has previously experienced it.

High-tension Leads. On the high-tension side of the ignition system we are dealing with high voltages which will "flash over" or take the line of least resistance whenever possible. The high-tension leads between the coil and the distributor and between the distributor cap and the sparking plugs must, therefore, be tested at intervals by doubling the cable between the fingers and examining the surface for the tiny cracks which indicate that perishing has begun. Alternatively a soft, swollen appearance of the insulation is characteristic of the deterioration caused by the action of oil or petrol. The modern plastic-covered high-tension cables, which are much more resistant to either form of failure, should always be chosen when the leads are renewed, although rubber-covered 7-mm ignition cable may still be offered by some garages.

On later models special high-tension ignition cables are fitted which act also as resistors to prevent interference by the ignition system with radio or television receivers. These cables must not be cut and no attempt should be made to fit new terminals to them. They should not be replaced by ordinary copper-cored cables.

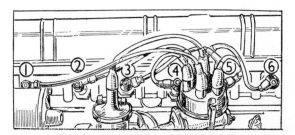

FIG. 26. SEQUENCE FOR CONNECTING SPARKING PLUG LEADS ON VITESSE SIX

THE IGNITION COIL

The remaining component in the ignition system—if we exclude the ignition switch and the battery—is the ignition coil (seen in Fig. 2), which converts the low-voltage current from the battery into the high-tension current that is needed to produce a spark at the plug points.

The ignition coil is a sealed, oil-insulated unit containing two windings, the primary—a relatively heavy winding consisting of a few hundred turns of wire which carries the battery current—and the secondary, which consists of many thousands of turns of fine wire, wound beneath the primary winding around an iron core. When the engine is running, current flows through the primary windings but is interrupted at the instant at which each spark is required by the opening of the contact

---

(Key to Fig. 27)

1. Nut	17. Distributor body
2. Lock-washer	18. Oil seal ring
3. Low-tension cable	19. Spacer
4. Capacitor (condenser)	20. Driving dog
5. Terminal stud	21. Rivet
6. Fixed contact	22. Clamp plate and bolt
7. Moving contact	23. Thrust washer
8. Nut	24. Tachometer (rev. counter) gear
9. Screw (fixed contact)	25. End cover
10. Rotor arm	26. Spring
11. Contact baseplate	27. Felt plug
12. Centrifugal action plate	28. Cap
13. Vacuum advance unit	29. Screw
14. Spacer	30. Cap clip
15. Oil-retaining felt	31. Setscrew
16. Felt-retaining clip	

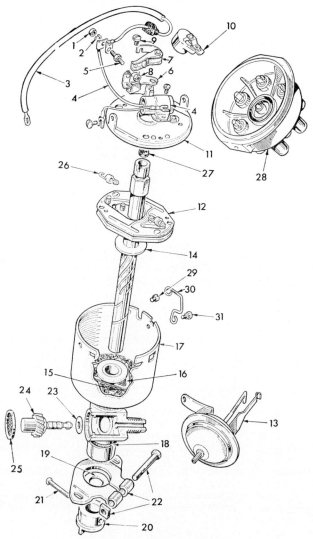

FIG. 27. TYPICAL DELCO-REMY IGNITION DISTRIBUTOR

A Lucas distributor is shown in Fig. 23.

KEY ON FACING PAGE

points in the distributor which form, in effect, an automatic on-off switch driven by the engine.

This induces a very high current in the secondary winding—it may reach a peak of 30,000 volts—but in practice the voltage continues to rise only until it is sufficient to cause a spark to jump across the sparking plug gap. The voltage required depends on a number of factors, such as the compression pressure existing in the combustion chamber at that moment, the air-fuel ratio of the mixture, the sparking plug temperature and the width of the gap.

The coil is the one item in the ignition system that usually requires little or no attention, apart from keeping the external surface clean— particularly the moulded cap. Remember that a current which reaches a peak of many thousands of volts will always try to find a leakage path from the central terminal to one of the low-tension terminals or to the earthed metal case of the coil. Moisture or greasy dirt is very liable to form such a conducting path.

A coil may appear to be perfectly satisfactory when cold or for a short period after the engine has been started, but may develop a partial or complete open-circuit in the windings when it has become thoroughly warmed-up, causing misfiring or ignition failure. As the coil will resume its normal action as soon as it cools down, this can often prove a very elusive fault to diagnose. When special test equipment is not available the best plan is to substitute temporarily a coil that is known to be in good condition.

The voltage provided by the standard ignition coil is, of course, adequate for all normal conditions but a high-voltage coil (such as the Runbaken) is a good investment, often providing better starting in cold weather, smoother and stronger pulling at low speeds and a better spark at high speeds, the higher price enabling the manufacturer to incorporate more efficient windings, better insulation and more effective heat dissipation.

Spark Intensifiers. Many so-called spark intensifiers consist, in fact, of nothing more than an auxiliary spark gap—two wood screws in a plastic housing—that is intended to be fitted in the main high-tension lead between the ignition coil and the distributor. Often the cost is out of all proportion to the real value of the device. Moreover the high voltage that is continuously imposed on the ignition system by the permanent spark gap may cause a breakdown in the insulation at some point.

The Norton ignition converter is, however, a notable exception to the general rule. This device, which is obtainable from Scrutton and Co., 97 Wanstead Park Road, Ilford, Essex, operates on an entirely different principle, by converting the normal ignition current into a high-frequency oscillating discharge. Now, a high-frequency current has some unusual characteristics. For example it treats an oiled-up plug insulator, or one that (in terms of ordinary high-tension current) is short-circuited by condensed moisture, as a far more formidable barrier than the air gap between the plug points! It is not surprising, therefore, that the Norton converter confers virtual immunity against difficult starting or misfiring caused by oiled-up plugs or condensation. Even under more normal conditions, the more effective spark usually results in smoother and more regular idling, better pulling and some improvement in fuel consumption.

IGNITION TIMING

A small alteration in the ignition timing—the instant at which the spark occurs in the combustion chamber—can have an appreciable effect on the performance and fuel consumption of the engine. Moreover the optimum timing at any moment depends on a number of factors which vary as running conditions change. The grade of fuel that is normally used also enters into the picture, "premium" or "super" fuels being less liable to detonate or pre-ignite than "regular" brands when the engine is pulling hard at low speeds, thus allowing the spark to be timed earlier than would otherwise be the case.

Micrometer Timing Control. On some distributors the static position of the contact-breaker baseplate can be varied over a small range of timing by rotating the knurled nut on the vacuum timing control without disturbing the main setting of the distributor. On all models except the Spitfire each of the divisions that registers with the edge of the housing represents a change in timing of 4 degrees at the crankshaft, so that the setting should not be altered more than say, half a division at a time. On the Spitfire distributor one click of the adjusting screw is equivalent to one degree. Clockwise rotation advances the ignition.

Obtaining Initial Setting. The initial setting is checked by slackening the clamping bolt beneath the distributor body and rotating the distributor in either direction, thus varying the position of the movable arm of the contact-breaker in relation to the cam; obviously, if the distributor is turned against the direction of rotation of the cam the spark will occur earlier, and vice versa. On reflection it will also be evident that altering the gap between the contact-breaker points will have a similar effect; increasing the gap will advance the ignition and decreasing it will retard. It is therefore important first to true-up the points and set the gap accurately.

The method of setting the timing on the different models is as follows—
Herald 948, 1200, 12/50, 13/60 *and Vitesse up to Engine No.* HB15000. Set the vernier scale fully retarded. On Herald models bring the engine to top-dead-centre by lining up a hole or mark on the rim of the crankshaft pulley with the pointer on the timing chain cover. On Vitesse models align the "O" mark of the scale engraved on the rim of the crankshaft vibration damper with the pointer on the timing cover.

Rotate the distributor clockwise until the contact-breaker points are just separating. Tighten the clamping bolt. The engine is now set to fire at top-dead-centre and the correct amount of advance can be given by turning the micrometer adjustment anti-clockwise until the correct number of divisions is visible on the scale. Each division is equivalent to four degrees. Therefore $2\frac{1}{4}$ divisions equals 9° B.T.D.C.; $2\frac{1}{2}$ divisions, 10°, and $3\frac{3}{4}$ divisions, 15°. The correct timing for each model is given on page 118.

Vitesse from Engine No. 15001. There is no micro-adjuster on the

FIG. 28. TIMING MARKS APPLIED TO FAN BELT DRIVING PULLEY
ON FOUR-CYLINDER ENGINES

distributor fitted to later Vitesse engines and it is therefore necessary to set the engine to the 10° mark before top-dead-centre on the scale engraved in the crankshaft damper rim. This mark must be aligned with the pointer on the timing case *before* the "O" mark reaches the pointer The distributor should then be rotated clockwise until the contact-breaker points are just breaking, when the clamping bolt can be tightened.

Spitfire. Set the distributor with the points just breaking at top-dead-centre as described for the Herald and turn the adjusting screw clockwise by the number of clicks equivalent to the ignition advance required. On this distributor each click is equivalent to one degree.

Checking Instant at which Points Separate. If the ignition is switched on, a small spark can be seen and heard to jump across the points as they separate. A more accurate method of timing is to connect a side-lamp bulb, mounted in a suitable holder, across the two low-tension terminals at the top of the ignition coil. When the points are closed the lamp will light up; at the instant that they open, it will be extinguished. When checking this point, keep a light finger pressure on the rotor in a clockwise direction to take up backlash in the drive.

Checking the Timing on the Road. The static setting should be regarded only as the starting point for a series of road tests during which the timing can be precisely adjusted by the micrometer control on the distributor to suit the condition of the engine and the fuel that will normally be used. The official recommendation is that the timing should be progressively advanced until the engine just shows signs of pinking under full throttle on a moderately steep hill. While this method gives quite good results with ordinary fuels, however, some premium fuels have such high anti-knock values that the possibility of over-advancing the engine before pinking occurs, cannot be entirely ruled out.

The method favoured by tuning enthusiasts is to make a series of tests, on a level road, noting carefully, by stop-watch readings, the time taken to accelerate from 20 m.p.h. to 40 m.p.h. in top gear, with the throttle fully open in each case and over the same stretch of road, so that each test is conducted under precisely similar conditions. The best ignition setting is that which results in the shortest time to accelerate over the speed range. This will also give the most economical fuel consumption.

Alternatively, start each test from a given point and note the point at which the higher speed is reached by reference to bushes by the roadside, fencing posts or similar identifying marks.

When altering the timing by the roadside, turn the micrometer adjuster or rotate the distributor body only a very small amount at a time. Take great care not to over-advance the timing, as this can damage the pistons and bearings.

4 The Carburettor and Petrol Pump

IF the simple maintenance described in this chapter and in Chapter 1 is conscientiously carried out, carburettor and fuel-system faults should seldom be experienced. If trouble does crop up, however—and the possibility cannot, of course, be entirely eliminated—the fault can usually be traced and cured without very much difficulty if the suggestions given at the end of this chapter are followed.

The engines are fitted with either Solex, Zenith-Stromberg or S.U. carburettors, the higher-performance Herald engines, the Spitfire and the Vitesse having twin-carburettor assemblies which give better mixture distribution between the cylinders and improved "breathing" at high speeds. The types of carburettors are listed in Chapter 7.

The three types of carburettors differ fundamentally in design and it is therefore necessary to consider each type separately, beginning with the Solex units.

SOLEX CARBURETTORS

The three basic types of Solex carburettor fitted to four- and six-cylinder engines are shown in Figs. 29–31. The illustrations of the Vitesse carburettor show the earlier type, which is fitted with an acceleration pump; but to improve hot starting, the pumps were omitted on later models, a blanking plate being fitted to each carburettor. This modification can be carried out by a Triumph dealer. It consists of removing the pump jets and fitting blanking plugs (or, on a do-it-yourself basis, sealing each jet with a spot of solder) disconnecting and removing the pump operating rods and removing the operating arms from the diaphragm covers by tapping out the pivot pins. The later jet settings given in Chapter 7 can also be adopted with advantage on earlier carburettors.

Apart from this modification, however, the jets listed for the range of carburettors represent the best compromise between performance and fuel economy and there is nothing to be gained from experimenting with different settings, except when the car is being used in countries in which there is a marked difference in the type of petrol available, in the atmospheric conditions or in the height above sea level at which most of the running is carried out. In such cases the advice of the local Triumph agent should be sought, as he will have the necessary experience of local conditions and of any changes in carburation that may be necessary to compensate for them.

Carburettor Adjustment. Considering first single-carburettor installations, the throttle-stop screw adjusts the opening of the throttle when the accelerator pedal is released and therefore regulates the slow-running speed. The richness of the slow-running mixture is determined by the volume-control screw, a greater volume of mixture being admitted, and the mixture correspondingly enriched, when the screw is turned anti-clockwise.

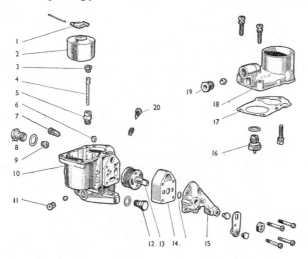

FIG. 29. SOLEX CARBURETTOR FITTED TO HERALD 948 c.c. AND "S"

1. Needle-valve lever	11. Ignition-control union
2. Float	12. Starter fuel jet
3. Air-correction jet	13. Starter-valve assembly
4. Emulsion tube	14. Starter-valve body
5. Emulsion tube head	15. Starter cover
6. Pilot air bleed	16. Needle valve
7. Pilot (slow-running) jet	17. Gasket
8. Main-jet holder	18. Float-chamber cover
9. Main jet	19. Fuel inlet union
10. Float-chamber body	

These screws are easily identified as they have knurled heads with screw-driver slots and are prevented from rotating accidentally by short coil springs.

To obtain the exact settings the engine should be at normal running temperature and the throttle-stop screw turned so that the engine will run just fast enough to prevent stalling. The volume-adjusting screw should then be screwed in or out until the engine runs evenly. The throttle-stop screw should now be readjusted if the engine is running too fast, followed by a further adjustment of the volume-adjusting screw. The operation should be repeated until satisfactory idling is obtained. Do not attempt to obtain too slow an idling speed. Small four-cylinder engines are not designed to tick-over at very low speeds. If the carburettor is adjusted to give a very slow tick-over when the engine is hot, stalling may be experienced when it is cold or when the clutch pedal is depressed.

If the mixture is too rich, the engine will run with a rhythmic beat and the exhaust may show dark smoke. If the mixture is too weak, the engine is likely to stall or spit-back when suddenly accelerated and the exhaust will sound irregular and "splashy."

The strength of the slow-running mixture considerably influences acceleration from low speeds. If there is a "flat spot" when the throttle is opened from the idling position, try the effect of slightly enriching the slow-running mixture; half a turn of the screw may be sufficient. It will probably be necessary to adjust the stop screw slightly to prevent "lumpy" idling, but an idling setting that is slightly on the rich side is an advantage.

Remember that it will be impossible to obtain good idling if ignition or mechanical faults exist (*see* page 75).

(*Key to Fig. 30*)

1. Screw	33. Nut
2. Strangler	34. Spring washer
3. Screw	35. Cable clip
4. Spring washer	36. Screw
5. Top cover	37. Abutment bracket
6. Gasket	38. Spring
7. Float	39. Solderless nipple
8. Air correction jet	40. Pinch screw
9. Econostat fuel jet	41. Pinch screw
10. Spraying bridge retaining screw	42. Pump cover and lever assembly
11. Body	43. Screw
12. Spraying bridge	44. Setscrew
13. Slow running adjustment screw	45. Non-return ball valve
14. Slow running fuel jet	46. Pump diaphragm
15. Spring	47. Diaphragm spring
16. Nut	48. Throttle butterfly
17. Throttle lever	49. Throttle spindle
18. Stop lever	50. Screw
19. Slotted washer	51. Main jet access plug
20. Strangler—inter-connection lever	52. Fibre washer
21. Spring	53. Main jet
22. Volume control screw	54. Pump chamber non-return valve body
23. Washer	55. Non-return ball valve
24. Spring	56. Fibre washer
25. Washer	57. Accelerator pump jet
26. Strangler inter-connection push rod	58. Pump chamber non-return valve
27. Split pin	59. Float lever
28. Strangler operating cam	60. Float lever pivot
29. Spring	61. Needle valve
30. Pivot bolt	62. Strangler cam follower and spindle
31. Accelerator pump push rod	63. Return spring
32. Circlip	64. Fibre washer

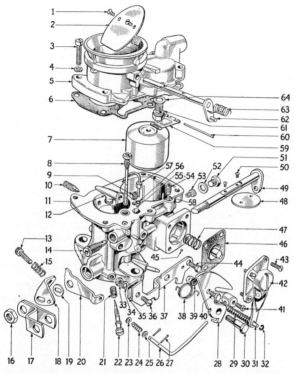

Fig. 30. Solex B30 PSE1 Fitted to Herald 1200 and 12/50

Cleaning the Jets. If the engine cannot be made to tick-over for any length of time, or stalls when decelerating, the slow-running or pilot jet may be blocked. Water or fine sediment may enter the float chamber and be drawn into any of the jets, in fact, causing erratic running or complete loss of power. The jets should, therefore, be removed occasionally for cleaning.

On the carburettors fitted to the 948 c.c. Herald and Herald "S", the jets which are most likely to need attention—the pilot or slow-running jet, the main jet and the starter jet—can be removed without dismantling the carburettor, as shown in Fig. 29.

In the case of the Herald 1200 and 12/50, however, only the slow-running jet can be unscrewed from outside the carburettor (see Fig. 30). To clean the main jet, econostat fuel jet and the air correction jet it will be necessary to remove the upper casting of the carburettor after taking off the air cleaner, disconnecting the fuel supply pipe and unscrewing the five screws that retain the top cover. When the float has been lifted out, the main jet will be seen at the base of the float bowl. The other jets are screwed into the upper face of the bowl. To unscrew the main jet, first remove the plug from the side of the bowl to allow a thin screwdriver to be passed through the hole to engage with the slot in the main jet.

On no account should the accelerator pedal or the accelerator pump lever be moved while the top cover is off. Otherwise the accelerator pump jet may be dislodged from its seating and the non-return valve ball may be ejected, possibly entering the inlet manifold through the carburettor choke tube, which would entail a good deal of dismantling before the ball could be retrieved.

Jets should be cleaned by washing them in petrol and blowing through them in the reverse direction to the normal flow of fuel. Never use wire to probe them. They are calibrated to very fine limits and engine performance and economy will suffer if the jet orifices are altered.

After cleaning the jets, of course, the slow-running adjustments should be reset if necessary.

Float Chamber and Float. The opportunity should be taken, when cleaning the jets, to clean out the float bowl. This can best be done by swilling it out with petrol to ensure that all sediment has been removed. After removing the toggle-arm that operates the petrol-supply needle-valve the float can be lifted out by using two short, hooked lengths of small-diameter wire.

The jet passages should be flushed out as thoroughly as possible. A plastic "lemon," filled with petrol, makes an inexpensive but effective flushing device.

Rich-mixture Device for Cold Starting. A much richer mixture than that required for normal running is needed when starting a cold engine, owing to condensation of the petrol mist on the interior surfaces of the inlet manifold, combustion chambers and cylinder walls. In the case of the carburettors fitted to the Herald 1200 and 12/50, the rich starting mixture is ensured by closing a flap valve in the air intake of the carburettor, thus allowing only a small amount of air to enter and at the same time creating a very strong suction on the petrol jets.

If you examine the exterior of your carburettor, however, you will see that the arm attached to the spindle of the pivoted flap is not operated directly by the starting control wire but rests on a pivoted cam plate. As the latter is rotated when the dashboard knob is pulled out, the projection on the flap-operating spindle follows it, under the action of a light coil spring. As soon as the engine fires, however, the rush of air through the carburettor intake tends to open the flap slightly against the tension of the spring, owing to the fact that the flap is slightly offset on its spindle, so that an unbalanced air pressure is set up. In this way the mixture strength is reduced as soon as the engine begins to run, preventing the cylinders being over-dosed with petrol which would wash away the lubricant and possibly swamp the sparking plugs, causing the engine to stall and resulting in considerable difficulty in restarting.

Because the flap valve is closed only by the pressure of the spring, however, any dirt or gum on the spindle may result in the valve failing to close fully, thus causing difficult starting in cold weather. If this trouble is suspected first check that the operating lever is following the cam plate when the knob on the dashboard is pulled out. If the spindle is sticking, work the lever by hand a few times while injecting thin oil (preferably graphited penetrating oil) into the spindle bearing on each side of the carburettor air intake, until the spindle is quite free and the valve snaps shut under the pressure of the spring.

Starting Carburettor. On the carburettor fitted to the Herald 948 c.c. and "S" engines and also on the early Vitesse, a different method of providing the rich starting mixture is adopted: a small, self-contained carburettor built into the main instrument and drawing its petrol supply from the main float chamber. The component parts can be seen in Figs. 29 and 31.

The throttle pedal should not be depressed when starting from cold as opening the throttle will destroy the suction created at the outlet from the starting carburettor. As with the strangler flap type of starting device, the starting carburettor is designed to weaken the mixture as soon as the engine fires and begins to run.

It will be seen that the only faults likely to cause trouble are incorrect adjustment of the wire from the dashboard control to the starting carburettor or blockage of the starting carburettor jet. In each case the remedy is obvious. Where the control wire is concerned, this should be clamped so that there is a slight free movement of the dashboard control before the slack is taken-up; on the other hand, if too much free movement is permitted the control valve may not be fully opened when the choke control is operated.

Acceleration Pump. The carburettors fitted to Triumph 1200 and 12/50 engines and to the earlier Vitesse Six, incorporate acceleration pumps which provide an enriched mixture whenever the accelerator pedal is depressed. On later Vitesse carburettors, however, this pump is not fitted; as mentioned earlier, it was found to be unnecessary and tended to cause difficult starting when the engine was hot if the accelerator pedal was depressed.

On any engine fitted with an acceleration pump, in fact, depressing the accelerator when starting a hot engine will inject an excessive amount of fuel into the inlet manifold, rendering it difficult or impossible to persuade the engine to fire. In such a case the only effective course is to press the accelerator slowly down to the fully-open position and to hold

(Key to Fig. 31)

1. Rear carburettor	40. Spring
2. Front carburettor	41. Throttle spindle
3. Fuel hose	42. Screws
4. Choke cable—inner	43. Throttle disc
5. Choke cable—outer	44. Gasket
6. Pinch bolt	45. Insulation gasket
7. Accelerator lever	46. Gasket
8. Plain washer	47. Starter jet
9. Nut	48. Washer
10. Plain washer	49. Jet block assembly
11. Coupling assembly	50. Gasket
12. Coupling rod	51. Emulsion tube
13. Spring washer	52. Carburettor body
14. Plain washer	53. Air correction jet
15. Nut	54. Distance piece
16. Pinch bolt	55. Split pins
17. Spring coupling	56. Plain washer
18. Screw and spring washer	57. Plain washer
19. Top cover	58. Nut
20. Gasket	59. Lever
21. Pinch screw	60. Split pins
22. Lever	61. Spring
23. Nut	62. Plain washer
24. Pinch screw	63. Push rod
25. Circlip	64. Idling mixture adjusting screw
26. Screw	65. Spring
27. Nipple	66. Idling mixture air bleed jet
28. Ball	67. Idling mixture fuel jet
29. Spring	68. Pump jet
30. Bolt	69. Screw
31. Fibre washer	70. Screw
32. Needle valve	71. Pump cover plate assembly
33. Pivot pin	72. Pump diaphragm
34. Float assembly	73. Spring
35. Starter cover	74. Fibre washer
36. Circlip	75. Screw
37. Starter body	76. Main jet
38. Disc valve	77. Main jet carrier
39. Idling speed adjusting screw	

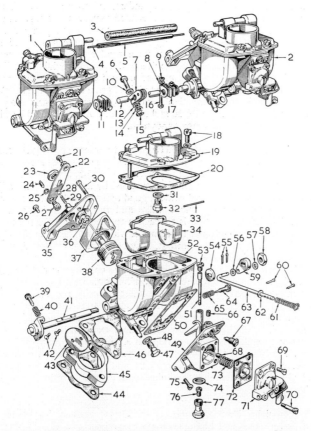

Fig. 31. Solex 32 PIH Carburettors Fitted to Earlier Vitesse
Blanking plates are fitted in place of the acceleration pump on later carburettors

it there while the engine is rotated by the starter motor, until the over-rich mixture has been cleared from the cylinders. As soon as the engine fires the accelerator should, of course, be released to prevent the engine racing.

When the carburettor is fitted with an acceleration pump and the engine does not accelerate strongly when the throttle is snapped open (assuming, of course, that it is at its normal running temperature), it is possible that the trouble may be due to the pump providing insufficient fuel. Faults to look for are a choked pump jet, a badly seating pump-non-return valve (usually due to a particle of grit on the valve seating) or a cracked or perforated pump diaphragm. The component parts of a pump are clearly shown in Figs. 29, 30 and 31 and dismantling should be within the capabilities of the average handyman.

Fast-idle Setting 1200 and 12/50 Engines. In order to provide the correct starting mixture the throttle must be opened slightly when the choke flap valve is closed. A lever on the flap valve is therefore interconnected with the throttle lever by a rod which is clamped by a setscrew. This adjustment should never be altered without good reason. Adjusting the correct relationship between the choke valve and throttle opening is a little tricky. The correct method is to slacken the setscrew, close the throttle valve on to a length of 0·027 in.-diameter wire placed between the edge of the throttle and carburettor throat, fully close the choke and tighten up the screw that clamps the interconnecting rod.

This can only be done, however, with the carburettor removed from the engine. In practice it is usually possible to find the correct setting by trial-and-error methods. Slacken the interconnecting rod clamping screw and start the engine from cold with the choke fully closed, by screwing in the idling speed adjusting screw until the engine fires and will continue to run, still with the choke closed, without excessive lumpiness or any tendency to stall through over-richness during the warming-up period. When a satisfactory fast-idle setting has been found, tighten the clamping screw. When the engine has warmed up and the choke control has been pushed fully home, readjust the idling speed control to restore the normal idling speed.

Synchronizing Twin Carburettors on Vitesse Engine. To obtain the best performance and fuel consumption, coupled with the silky-smooth running of which the Vitesse engine is capable, the two carburettors must be carefully synchronized. Before doing this, check that the ignition timing is correctly set as described in Chapter 3, adjust the valve clearances (Chapter 1), make sure that both operating levers on the starting carburettors return to the fully-closed position and remove and blow through the carburettor jets to ensure that they are unobstructed.

While the carburettors top covers are off, invert each float chamber lid and place a ruler across the machined face above the needle valve. The top of the valve should just touch the edge of the ruler. If it is more than 0·020 in. beneath the edge, fit an additional washer, Solex Part No. 10593, beneath the valve.

Make sure that the floats are not dented or punctured and that the arm connecting each pair is not bent. The easiest way to check the float arms is to place each assembly in turn on an oblong piece of wood, 2 in. long, $1\frac{1}{2}$ in. wide and $\frac{1}{2}$ in. thick, with all sides squared up. The pivot pin boss of the arm must lie squarely on the edge of the block, the tops of the

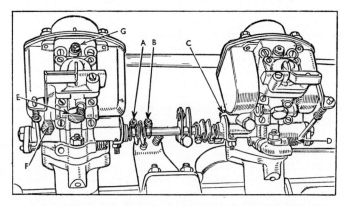

FIG. 32. THE TWIN CARBURETTOR ASSEMBLY ON EARLIER VITESSE ENGINES

The later Solex carburettors are similar, but are not fitted with acceleration pumps

A, B. Clamping bolts on throttle rods	*E.* Main jet
C. Idling speed adjustment	*F.* Starter jet
D. Idling mixture adjustment	*G.* Pilot jet

floats must be parallel with the upper edge of the block and the same distance below it, while the inner sides of the floats must also be parallel with the sides of the block. If necessary, carefully bend the arms to bring the floats into the correct position.

When the carburettors have been reassembled start the engine and let it run until it is at its normal temperature. Then slacken the clamping bolts on the flexible linkage between the throttles and disconnect the throttle return spring.

Adjust each carburettor separately by unscrewing both the slow-running speed adjusting screws until they are clear of their stops and making sure that the throttles are closed by pressing gently on the screw heads. Retighten the connecting linkage between the carburettors, making sure that both throttles remain closed. The securing bolts on the front and rear couplings should be arranged at 90 deg. to each other as shown in Fig. 31.

Gently screw the mixture control screws clockwise until they touch their seatings and then unscrew each by one full turn. Reconnect the throttle return spring.

Now screw in each slow-running speed adjusting screw until it just touches the stop on the carburettor body and then turn each through one further complete turn. Start the engine and adjust both screws *by an exactly equal amount* until the engine is idling at about 600–650 r.p.m.

Unscrew each mixture control screw a quarter of a turn at a time until the engine begins to "hunt," indicating over-richness. Screw in the mixture screws, again by equal amounts, until the hunting just disappears and the engine idles smoothly. If the idling speed has now increased, reduce it to about 600–650 r.p.m. by adjusting each slow-running screw by an equal amount. Do not be tempted to try to obtain a very slow tick-over. The high compression ratios and the valve timings used on modern engines call for a fairly brisk idling speed if the risk of the engine stalling when the throttle is suddenly closed is to be avoided.

S.U. CARBURETTORS

The twin-carburettor engines fitted to some Herald models and to the Spitfire have two S.U. carburettors, the earlier design being shown in Fig. 33 and the later type in Fig. 34. As far as servicing and adjustment are concerned the two types are very similar, the main difference being that in the case of the later, HS2 carburettor, the jet assembly is simpler than the earlier design, the jet consisting of a metal tube sliding in a simple bearing bush and fed with fuel through a nylon tube. Consequently the cork glands and sealing washers, which were apt to be sources of petrol leakage on the earlier type of carburettor, are not required. The design of the float chamber and float is also different but the notes on maintenance and tuning which follow are broadly applicable to both designs.

Each carburettor serves two cylinders of the engine. A balance pipe connects the inlet pipes but it cannot be too strongly emphasized that the performance, economy and smoothness of the engine depend on correct setting and synchronization of the carburettors.

If the engine is running satisfactorily, therefore, and the carburettors have been correctly set by an experienced mechanic, the owner should not attempt to alter any of the adjustments. It is very easy to put the carburettors out of synchronization and considerable experience is required to readjust them correctly.

Assuming, however, that such faults as lack of speed or poor acceleration, excessive fuel consumption or rough or uneven running, cannot be traced to ignition or mechanical faults, the carburettors may be checked and adjusted. If the instructions below are carefully followed, satisfactory performance should be restored.

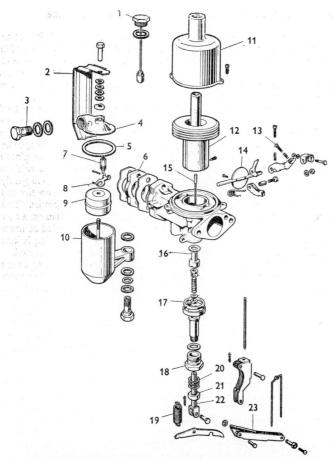

Fig. 33. Earlier S.U. Carburettor Dismantled

1. Damper piston
2. Heat shield
3. Fuel inlet-union
4. Float-chamber cover
5. Gasket
6. Heat-insulating washer
7. Needle valve
8. Needle-valve lever
9. Float
10. Float chamber
11. Suction chamber
12. Piston

13. Fast-idle adjustment
14. Throttle
15. Jet needle
16. Upper jet bearing
17. Jet gland
18. Jet locking sleeve
19. Jet-lever return spring
20. Jet-adjusting locking spring
21. Jet-adjusting nut
22. Jet-head
23. Jet-control lever

When the air cleaner and its manifold have been removed, it will be seen that each carburettor consists of a domed suction chamber which contains a sliding piston, visible when viewed through the air intake of the carburettor. This piston should slide freely and should fall onto its seating with a soft metallic click when released. A sticking piston is a likely cause of incorrect carburation.

The piston should not rise without resistance, since the upper part of the suction chamber contains an oil-filled damper which regulates the speed at which the piston rises. The first step, therefore, is to unscrew the cap nuts from the tops of the suction chambers, withdraw each spindle and damper plunger carefully, and fill the hollow section of the piston rod with engine oil of SAE 20W/50 viscosity, to within about half an inch of the top of drilling. The damper plunger can then be pressed gently but firmly into the oil-filled chamber until it is possible to screw the cap firmly home. Care must be taken not to bend the plunger spindle. This attention will normally be required about once every 3,000 miles on a new carburettor but, when the parts become worn, it may be needed at more frequent intervals. A symptom that the damper requires refilling is lack of acceleration and a tendency to spit-back when the throttle is opened.

There is one further point which deserves mention, before turning to the subject of carburettor servicing. The float chambers of the carburettors are rather close to the cylinder head and exhaust manifold, and this can cause vaporization of the fuel when the engine is hot. If difficult starting is experienced with a hot engine, a probable cure is to fit one-inch thick fibre packing pieces between the carburettors and the inlet manifold flanges. It will be necessary to substitute longer studs, of course, so the best plan is to have a word with your Standard-Triumph dealer regarding this modification.

Removing and Refitting the Pistons. Proceeding with a check of the carburettors, if attention to the dashpots does not improve matters, it will be necessary to remove the suction chambers by undoing the securing screws. The chamber should be lifted off the piston carefully and placed on a sheet of clean paper on the bench, since it is important to avoid the risk of any grit entering the parts. The piston can then be lifted out, when it will be seen that, at its lower extremity, a tapered needle is clamped by a setscrew. Great care must be taken not to bend this needle and it is most important that the point at which the slight taper changes suddenly to a larger section should be flush with the base of the piston. It is also important that both needles should protrude from the pistons by exactly the same amount.

On looking down into the body of the carburettor the top of the tubular brass jet will be visible. The jet adjusting nut (Fig. 35) should be turned until the jet is just level with the jet bridge.

At this stage the operation of the carburettor will be evident. The tapered needle passes into the jet. The piston, which is a reasonably airtight fit in the suction chamber, is subject to variations in the depression or semi-vacuum present in the induction manifold when the engine is running, so that it is raised and lowered to a varying extent which will depend on the throttle opening and the load on the engine. As the piston is raised, more air is allowed to pass between the piston and the throat of the carburettor, and at the same time the needle is withdrawn from the jet so that more petrol can mix with the air. In this manner the mixture is automatically regulated for all running conditions and, owing to the comparatively large bore of the jet, troubles caused by blockage of the jet on normal carburettors are seldom experienced on the S.U.

Continuing with the systematic check, after both jets have been adjusted by the jet adjusting nuts to bring them exactly level with the bridges in the carburettors, the pistons should be cleaned with a petrol-soaked cloth and the interiors of the suction chambers should be similarly wiped clean and allowed to dry. The grooved surfaces of the pistons must *not* be lubricated. Only a spot of oil should be applied to the polished piston rod. The pistons, each mated to its own suction chamber, can then be replaced, again taking care not to bend the jet needles, and the suction chambers refitted.

Centring the Jets. When the retaining screws have been tightened down evenly, the piston should be tested for freedom. If it does not fall freely on to the bridge-piece when the jet is fully up but does so when the jet is withdrawn by moving the choke control lever, the indication is that the jet is not correctly centred.

A large proportion of the carburettors returned to the S.U. works as defective are found on examination to be suffering from nothing more serious than this fault, which is easily rectified.

When the piston is at its lowest point and the jet is in its normal running position, only a very small radial clearance exists between the tapered needle and the opening in the jet. The assembly is, therefore, permitted a small amount of radial movement in order to allow it to be aligned with the jet, when it can be locked in position by means of a screwed sleeve, the hexagonal head of which can be seen at the base of the jet housing, above the spring that locks the jet adjusting nut.

The operation consists simply of unhooking the return spring and disconnecting the jet control lever from the base of the jet, withdrawing the jet completely and removing the adjusting nut and locking spring. The nut should then be replaced, without the spring, and screwed up as far as possible so that when the jet is slid in position it will be raised well above the normal level. The jet locking sleeve should now be slackened just sufficiently to free the jet assembly and the piston should be raised and lowered several times until it falls freely. The jet locking sleeve

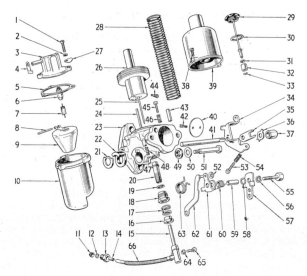

FIG. 34. S.U. TYPE HS2 CARBURETTOR FITTED TO SPITFIRE

1. Screw
2. Spring washer
3. Float chamber lid
4. Breather hole shroud
5. Gasket
6. Needle valve body
7. Needle valve
8. Float spindle
9. Float
10. Float chamber
11. Cup
12. Washer
13. Union nut
14. Sleeve
15. Jet
16. Adjusting nut
17. Spring
18. Jet retaining sleeve
19. Washer
20. Jet holder
21. Washer
22. Rubber seal
23. Main body
24. Lifting pin
25. Needle
26. Piston
27. Identification plate
28. Spring
29. Damper cap nut
30. Washer
31. Washer
32. Damper plunger
33. Circlip

34. Throttle adjusting bracket
35. Throttle fork
36. Lock tab
37. Nut
38. Screw
39. Vacuum chamber
40. Throttle disc
41. Throttle spindle
42. Screw
43. Mixture enrichment cable abutment
44. Needle retaining screw
45. Throttle stop screw
46. Spring
47. Circlip
48. Spring
49. Rubber seal
50. Plain washer
51. Bolt
52. Circlip
53. Fast-idle screw
54. Spring
55. Bolt
56. Spring washer
57. Cam lever
58. Distance washer
59. Tube
60. Return spring
61. Pick-up lever
62. Jet lever
63. Return spring
64. Shouldered washer
65. Screw
66. Flexible pipe

should then be tightened firmly and a test made to ensure that the piston is still free. It may be necessary to repeat these operations several times. If, after several attempts, it is impossible to prevent the needle binding in the jet, the needle is probably bent and must be renewed.

After the adjusting nut locking spring has been fitted, the mixture adjustment should be set as described below.

FIG. 35. EARLIER S.U. CARBURETTOR ADJUSTMENTS

1. Fast-idle adjustment
2. Throttle-stop screw
3. Throttle-interconnecting clamp
4. Jet-control lever
5. Jet-adjusting nut
6. Piston

Adjusting the Carburettors. Assuming that the piston falls freely, the dashpot chamber should be filled with oil as previously described and the other carburettor assembled in a similar manner.

The clamping screw and fast-idle adjusting screws (Figs. 33–5) should now be unscrewed to allow both throttles to close completely and independently. Slacken the clamping screws in the jet-control levers sufficiently to free the mixture-control cables.

As with all S.U. carburettors, the initial adjustment of the mixture quality—i.e. richness or weakness—at slow-running speeds determines the mixture over the whole of the speed range. It must be emphasized that on no account should any attempt be made to adjust the mixture strength at any speed other than the normal idling speed of about 500 r.p.m.; that is, at a reasonably fast tick-over.

With the jet-adjusting nuts unscrewed a few turns and the throttle stop screwed down so that each throttle is opened very slightly, the engine can be started and allowed to warm up. When it has attained the normal running temperature the idling speed should be adjusted by turning the throttle stop-screws.

At this stage it is particularly important to make sure that each carburettor is obtaining the same quantity of mixture; otherwise it will be impossible to regulate the mixture richness correctly between the two carburettors. This fault is probably the cause of most of the troubles experienced in synchronizing twin carburettors.

The most effective method is to listen to the hiss at the air intake, while adjusting the slow-running screws a fraction of a turn at a time until the intensity of the hiss is the same on both intakes. One end of a length of rubber tubing may be held to the ear while the other end is placed at exactly the same spot in each air intake. Much more effective results can be obtained, however, by using a child's toy stethoscope, which can be obtained quite inexpensively from many toy dealers. This little instrument is not only surprisingly effective in enabling the intensity of the hiss to be adjusted with great accuracy but can also be used subsequently to diagnose engine noises—for example, to identify a noisy tappet.

Assuming that both carburettors are drawing exactly the same amount of mixture, the jet-adjusting nuts must now be rotated a little at a time in order to enrich or weaken the mixture on each carburettor until a satisfactory exhaust note is obtained. This must be regular, free from "splashy" misfiring, or a rhythmic beat with signs of black smoke. The former indicates too weak a mixture while the latter is a sign that the mixture is too rich.

Checking Mixture Strength. The strength of the mixture delivered by each carburettor should be checked by lifting the piston $\frac{1}{32}-\frac{1}{16}$ in. with the tip of a penknife. When this is done the engine speed should remain substantially the same. If the engine speed increases, the carburettor is set too rich and the jet-adjusting nut must be screwed up slightly. If, on the other hand, the engine speed decreases, the jet-adjusting nut must be screwed further down.

It is important not to lift the piston too far, as may happen if the lifting plunger is employed. If the piston is lifted appreciably—say, $\frac{1}{4}$ in.—then that carburettor will be put partly out of action and the engine will run on the other carburettor. Under these conditions the engine should continue to run, but rather "bumpily." If it stalls, then the *opposite* carburettor to the one on which the piston is lifted is too weak. If the engine speeds-up and continues to run at a higher speed, then the *opposite* carburettor to that on which the piston is lifted is too rich. This point is stressed since the indications are opposite to those obtained when a piston is lifted only very slightly. It is best, therefore, to measure the thickness of the tip of a penknife blade and to slide it carefully between the piston and the jet bridge, just far enough to give the recommended lift of $\frac{1}{32}-\frac{1}{16}$ in.

The lifting-pin test can be used, however, when the air cleaner and air manifold are fitted, in which case the safest plan is to lift each plunger to the limit of its travel and to adjust the mixture strength on the other carburettor. If the idling speed increases when the mixture is correctly adjusted, it will be necessary to unscrew each slow-running screw by an *exactly similar amount* to restore the desired tick-over. At this point it is worth mentioning, however, that it will not necessarily be possible to maintain the jet-adjusting nuts in exact synchronization. When the correct mixture setting has been obtained, it may be found that one nut is as much as a turn or two turns further down than the other. This apparent discrepancy is well within normal variations, even on new carburettors, and is influenced by such factors as the exactly similar positioning of each jet needle in its piston or, on older carburettors, unequal wear on individual parts.

When the foregoing adjustments have been satisfactorily completed, the screw on the throttle interconnecting clamp should be fully tightened, making sure that each throttle stop-screw is held against its stop. The screws on the mixture-control levers can then be tightened-up. Make sure that there is a slight amount of slackness in the mixture control wire when the dashboard knob is pushed fully home, so that each jet head is firmly in contact with its adjusting nut, and that the jet levers move to the same extent when the control is pulled out.

It finally remains to set the fast-idle screw (shown in Figs. 33–5) to give the correct increase in idling speed when the mixture control is in use. There should be a gap of about 0·015 in. between the tip of the screw and the rocker lever, but it is as well to check this adjustment when the engine is first started from cold. The idling speed, with the mixture control fully pulled out, should not be excessively high but should be sufficient to prevent lumpy running and any tendency to stall during the warming-up period. Remember that this adjustment must be reset whenever the normal slow-running speed adjustment is altered.

ZENITH–STROMBERG CARBURETTORS

In operating principles, these carburettors, fitted to the Herald 13/60 and the later Vitesse models are basically similar to the S.U. type; but, as will seen from Fig. 36, they differ considerably in detailed design.

The mixture strength is regulated by a tapered needle (11) in the base of a piston (termed an air valve) (9) which rises and falls in response to engine speed and throttle opening, but in place of the metal disc used in the S.U., a flexible diaphragm (8) is attached to the top of the piston. The method of enriching the mixture for cold starting is also different. When the control is operated it rotates a starter bar (28) which has a flat milled on it. This lifts the air valve and needle, increasing the clearance between the needle and the jet. At the same time a cam on the air valve lever opens the throttle slightly to provide a higher idling speed than normal.

When the engine has fired and is beginning to warm up, the mixture control should be pushed in gradually in order to reduce the mixture strength and the amount of fast-idle throttle opening. It should be fully home by the time that normal running temperature is attained.

The movement of the air valve is damped by an oil-filled dashpot and a small plunger (12), which is again similar to the S.U. arrangement. This must be kept topped-up with SAE 20 engine oil to within $\frac{1}{4}$ in. of the end of the hollow guide rod. If the damper is allowed to become dry, or a thin machine oil is used to top it up, a flat-spot will be experienced when accelerating and the engine may spit back through the carburettor if the throttle is opened suddenly.

Setting the Idling Adjustments. The throttle-stop screw (29 in Fig. 36) controls the idling speed and the jet-adjusting screw (44) regulates the mixture strength. When turned clockwise it weakens the mixture.

It is best to begin the adjustment from a standard datum point. Bring the engine up to its normal working temperature, remove the air cleaner, unscrew and remove the hydraulic dashpot plunger from one carburettor and insert a pencil in the bore so that the air valve can be held down on to its seating on the bridge in the throttle passage.

Screw the jet-adjustment screw upwards—the edge of a coin is ideal for this purpose—until the jet just contacts the underside of the air valve. Then screw the adjusting screw down by three turns. Top-up the dashpot, refit the hydraulic damper and carry out the same procedure on the other carburettor.

Start the engine, run it until it has regained its normal temperature and then adjust each stop screw to give smooth idling at a speed of 600–650 r.p.m. There should be an equal hiss from the intakes of both carburettors. If the exhaust note is irregular, lift the air valve of one carburettor a very small amount—*not exceeding* $\frac{1}{32}$ in.—with the tip of a penknife blade or a thin screwdriver.

If the engine speed rises appreciably, the mixture supplied by that carburettor is too rich. If the engine stops, the mixture is too weak. When each carburettor is properly adjusted, the engine speed will either remain constant or will fall very slightly when each air valve is lifted.

Synchronizing the Carburettors. If the synchronization of twin-carburettors has been upset—for example, when they have been removed from the engine—the two throttles can be resynchronized by loosening the clamping bolts (38) on the throttle spindle couplings, unscrewing each throttle stop screw to allow the throttle to close completely and then tightening the clamping bolts on the couplings, while taking great care not to disturb the settings of the throttles.

Each throttle stop screw should now be screwed in until its tip just contacts the stop lever on the throttle spindle. From this point, rotate the stop screws one complete turn. This provides the basis from which final very careful adjustment of each screw can be made, in conjunction with the mixture adjustments described earlier, to provide even, regular idling. It will be appreciated that although each throttle stop screw must normally be rotated by the same amount in order to keep the two carburettors in step, as it were, slight differences in efficiency between individual cylinders, the valve gear, sparking plugs and induction and exhaust tracts, usually mean that the settings on each carburettor for best results are not precisely the same.

Checking the Float Chamber Level. If it is not possible to obtain smooth idling after carrying out the adjustment just described, the trouble may be due to incorrect petrol levels in the float chambers of the carburettors. This can be checked by removing each carburettor from the engine, taking off the float chamber and inverting the carburettor so that the highest point of the float (51) above the face of the main body can be measured when the needle valve is resting on its seating. The correct height is 18 mm.

If necessary, reset the level of the float by carefully bending the tag that makes contact with the end of the needle valve (6). Alternatively, the addition of a thin fibre washer beneath the needle-valve seating (56) will effectively lower the fuel level and will cure symptoms of over-richness caused by slight wear on the valve and seating. If correct setting of the float does not cure over-richness or flooding, however, the wisest plan is to renew the needle valve assembly in each carburettor. These are not expensive items and do not have an unlimited life.

Centralizing the Jet. As with S.U. carburettors, difficult starting and other carburettor troubles can be caused by a sticking air valve. This can be checked by lifting the valve with the spring-loaded pin (41) beneath the suction chamber housing. If the valve does not fall freely, it is a straightforward matter to remove it and clean the sliding portion and the bore in which it works. Use only petrol or paraffin. Do not lubricate the valve and don't be tempted to use emery cloth or metal polish to brighten it up, as the clearance between the valve and the bore is fairly critical.

If, on reassembly, the valve still does not fall freely, either the needle may be bent or the jet may not be central. In either event the needle will be rubbing against the side of the bore of the jet and the remedy is either

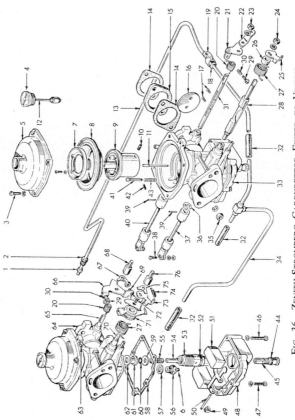

Fig. 36. Zenith-Stromberg Carburettor Fitted to Vitesse

(Key on Page 75)

to fit a new needle, with its shoulder flush with the lower face of the air valve, or to re-centralize the jet.

The latter job entails lifting the air valve and screwing up the jet-adjusting nut until the jet is slightly above the level of the bridge. Slacken the hexagon at the base of the jet bush screw (53). Half-a-turn should be sufficient to free the jet bush (61) and allow the jet to centralize itself around the needle when the air valve is allowed to fall. Carefully tighten the hexagon, while checking that the needle is still free, as indicated by a sharp click when the base of the air valve strikes the bridge.

After this adjustment the idling settings must be restored as described earlier.

Diagnosing Faults. When difficult starting, heavy fuel consumption, misfiring and loss of power are experienced, the carburettor may not necessarily be at fault. The trouble may be due to a combination of other faults, such as ignition system troubles, badly seating valves, worn piston rings and cylinders, leaking cylinder-head gaskets, defective inlet manifold

---

(Key to Fig. 36)

1. Sleeve
2. Union nut
3. Cover screw
4. Damper filler plug
5. Cover
6. Needle valve
7. Diaphragm retaining ring
8. Diaphragm
9. Air valve
10. Needle locking screw
11. Jet needle
12. Damper spindle
13. Fuel pipe
14. Gasket
15. Heat insulator
16. Throttle plate
17. Throttle screws
18. Grommet
19. Bracket
20. Spring
21. Throttle stop
22. Throttle lever
23. Nut
24. Nut
25. Lever
26. Bush
27. Starter bar spring
28. Starter bar
29. Throttle stop screw
30. Spring
31. Throttle spindle
32. Fuel pipe connection
33. Float chamber
34. Pipe
35. Nut
36. Retaining ring
37. Coupling
38. Bolt
39. Pin
40. Coupling
41. Piston lifting pin
42. Clip
43. Spring
44. Sealing ring
45. Jet adjusting screw
46. Screw (long)
47. Screw (short)
48. Float chamber
49. Clip
50. Pin
51. Float assembly
52. Sealing ring
53. Jet bush screw
54. Jet
55. Spring
56. Needle seat
57. Washer
58. Gasket
59. Washer
60. Sealing ring
61. Jet bush
62. Washer
63. Screw
64. Body
65. Spindle
66. Stop
67. Washer
68. Nut
69. Fast-idling adjusting screw
70. Starter bar
71. Fast-idle lever
72. Screw
73. Lever
74. Spring
75. Washer
76. Nut

or carburettor gaskets and mechanical faults, all of which can adversely affect performance and fuel consumption and can cause difficult starting.

Before blaming the carburettor, therefore, a general check should be made on the mechanical condition of the engine and the car as a whole. An authorized Standard-Triumph dealer has the necessary equipment to carry out such checks quickly and efficiently.

THE PETROL PUMP

The petrol pump requires little attention, other than to keep the filter free from dirt and sediment. An occasional check should be made to ensure that the fuel pipe unions are tight.

The pump is fitted with an external hand-operating lever. If the car has been out of use for several days most of the petrol will have evaporated from the carburettor float chamber: to avoid having to rotate the engine by the starter motor or handle until the float chamber has been refilled, the priming lever can be operated until the pumping action ceases. If there is no resistance to the movement of the lever initially, the indication is that the eccentric on the camshaft that operates the petrol pump is in contact with the pump lever. The engine should be given approximately one complete turn with the starting handle, when the priming lever should operate normally. In the summer, and with a well-charged battery, there is little object in using the primer: but in the winter it can save a considerable drain on the battery and ensure a much quicker start than would otherwise be the case.

If the pump fails to operate, no attempt should be made to dismantle it. Your Standard-Triumph dealer or agent will be able to supply and fit a reconditioned, guaranteed pump in exchange for the faulty unit.

5 Brake Adjustment and Maintenance

ALL models are fitted with Girling hydraulic brakes. The Herald models have drum brakes at front and rear in which the fluid pressure, generated in the master cylinder when the brake pedal is depressed, is transmitted by pipelines to small pistons, working in cylinders attached to the brake backplates. These pistons force the friction-lined brake shoes outwards against the drums.

In the case of the Herald 13/60, Spitfire and Vitesse, however, the front brakes are of the disc type, consisting of a pair of operating pistons housed in cylinders in a caliper which straddles a steel disc attached to the wheel hub. When fluid pressure is generated in the braking system the pistons press pads faced with friction material against the sides of the steel disc, in much the same manner that caliper cycle brakes force the brake blocks against the edge of the wheel rim. The general arrangement can be seen in Fig. 39. Disc brakes are self-adjusting and need no servicing until the time comes to renew the friction pads as described on page 83.

The rear brake shoes can also be moved outwards mechanically, by leverage applied by short levers coupled by cables to the handbrake, thus providing an effective parking brake and also a second line of defence in the unlikely event of the hydraulic system failing.

An inherent advantage of a hydraulic braking system is that the pressure generated in the master cylinder is transmitted equally throughout the system, thus providing balanced braking. If the friction of one or more of the brake linings or friction pads is reduced by oil or grease, however—as the result, for example, of a defective hub oil seal—unbalanced braking is bound to result.

Spitfire Mark 3 cars exported to the U.S.A. have a dual-line breaking system which supplies hydraulic pressure independently to the front and rear brakes. One pair of brakes will therefore continue to operate if the other pair should fail for any reason—for example, if pressure is lost due to damage to the pipeline or failure of a rubber seal.

The master cylinder is of the "tandem" type and contains two pistons, supplied from a common hydraulic reservoir. A pressure-differential warning switch is included in the system to illuminate a warning light on the dashboard if one half of the braking system should fail. This consists of a simple shuttle valve which operates a plunger switch if it is moved from its central position by a difference in pressure in the pipelines serving the front and rear brakes.

The dual-line system requires the same maintenance as the standard braking system.

Routine Maintenance. The only routine attention required (at 6,000-mile intervals) is to check the level of the fluid in the master cylinder reservoir and to top it up to within $\frac{1}{2}$ in. of the bottom of the filler neck, but not higher. Use only Girling fluid or an alternative fluid that conforms to SAE Specification 70R3.

If the level of the fluid in the reservoir is allowed to fall too low, air may enter the system, causing a "spongy" feel when the brake pedal is depressed and also a considerable reduction in braking power. If this trouble is suspected, the brakes should be "bled" as described on page 80.

Brake Adjustment. When the brake pedal must be depressed almost to the floorboard before the brakes are fully applied, the brake shoes must be adjusted to compensate for wear of the friction linings.

Before beginning work, first make sure that the tyres are inflated to the correct pressure and that there is no excessive bearing "play" in the front wheel bearings.

Jack-up the car to allow each wheel to be adjusted in turn, and check that the wheel rotates freely. The handbrake, of course, should be in the fully-released position when adjusting the rear brakes, at least one other wheel being securely chocked to prevent movement.

There are two square-headed adjusters at the "twelve o'clock" and "six o'clock" positions on the backplate of each front brake, enabling the two brake shoes to be adjusted individually. Spin the wheel and tighten up each adjuster by turning it clockwise until the shoes are locked on the drum, and then slacken back the adjuster one or two "clicks" and make sure that the wheel rotates freely. This adjustment should be done with the brake drums cold. Repeat this procedure with the other adjusters, but remember that there is only *one* adjuster on each rear brake, at the "six o'clock" position. There is a constant drag on the rear wheels owing to the resistance of the differential and axle oil; do not mistake this for brake shoe friction.

The brakes should now be tested on the road. A traffic-free stretch with a dry surface, preferably uncambered, should be selected for the purpose. The brakes should be applied hard at about 30 m.p.h. and the braking marks should be examined to determine whether any wheel is locking before the remainder. It should also be noted whether there is a tendency to pull towards one side of the road.

If it is found that the brakes are inefficient or unbalanced, the cause is most probably grease on the linings. It is extremely important that the linings should be kept free from grease and oil. The use of correct front

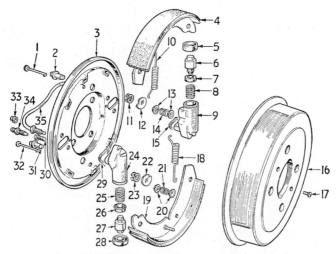

FIG. 37. A FRONT BRAKE ASSEMBLY AS IT WOULD APPEAR WHEN REMOVED AND DISMANTLED

1. Steady pin
2. Adjuster shank
3. Backplate
4. Brake shoe
5. Dust excluder
6. Piston
7. Seal
8. Spring
9. Wheel cylinder
10. Return spring
11. Spring
12. Adjuster cam
13. Steady-pin cups
14. Spring
15. Seal
16. Brake drum
17. Countersunk screw
18. Return spring
19. Brake shoe
20. Steady-pin cups
21. Spring
22. Adjuster cam
23. Spring
24. Wheel cylinder
25. Spring
26. Seal
27. Piston
28. Dust excluder
29. Seal
30. Screw
31. Adjuster shank
32. Steady-pin
33. Dust cap
34. Bleed screw
35. Bridge pipe

wheel bearing lubricant and care not to overfill the back axle, as well as replacing grease retainers when leakage is indicated, will help to maintain braking efficiency. If the linings are badly saturated with grease or oil, new, relined brake shoes should be fitted.

Bleeding the Brakes. If, as mentioned earlier, the level of the fluid in the reservoir is allowed to fall too low—or if a pipeline union is disconnected or slackens off—air will enter the braking system, necessitating the process known as "bleeding."

A nipple that incorporates a valve will be found on each backplate. Remove the rubber dust cap and attach a rubber or transparent plastic tube to one of the nipples, passing it through a box or ring spanner that fits the hexagon on the nipple, and submerge the free end of the tube in a little brake fluid in a clean glass jar. Open the bleeder screw one complete turn. Depress the pedal through its full stroke, followed by two or three short, rapid strokes. Then allow the pedal to return to its stop unaided. This pumping action should be repeated with a slight pause between each operation. A watch should be kept on the flow of liquid into the jar and when air bubbles cease to appear, the pedal should be held down firmly and the bleeder screw securely tightened. Repeat this operation on all wheel cylinders.

When a dual-line braking system is fitted, if both the front and the rear brakes are to be bled, begin with the rear brakes Turn the brake adjusters to lock the shoes against the drums and readjust the brakes when bleeding has been completed.

The brake pedal must be pressed gently and allowed to return slowly. It should not be pushed to the end of its travel or depressed rapidly, as this will cause the shuttle valve (described on page 78) to move and operate the warning-light switch. If this does happen, close the bleed screw on the brake that is being bled and open the bleed screw at the opposite end of the car. Switch on the ignition (do not start the engine). The brake warning light will now be illuminated and steady pressure should be applied to the brake pedal until the brake light goes dim and the oil warning light comes on. It is possible to feel a click through the pedal as the shuttle valve moves to the central position. If the pedal is pressed too hard, the valve will be moved to the opposite extreme and the operation just described will have to be reversed. Don't forget to tighten the bleed screw after centralizing the valve.

Handbrake Adjustment. Normally, adjustment at the rear brake shoes will automatically take up any excessive free movement on the handbrake lever. In time, however, the handbrake cable will stretch. It is then necessary to take up the slack by shortening the cable at the point at which it is attached to the operating lever on the backplate of the right-hand brake. On later models both ends of the cable are adjustable, enabling a greater degree of cable stretch to be taken up. On these models it is easier to carry out the adjustment at the point at which the cable is attached to the handbrake lever, after removing the sealing cover from the propellor shaft tunnel. Remember however, that excessive travel of the handbrake when the rear brake shoes are correctly adjusted is often an indication that the brake linings are nearing (or have reached) the end of their useful life.

Relining the Brakes. Dismantling drum-type brakes is quite straightforward. After jacking-up the car and removing the wheel, slacken off the

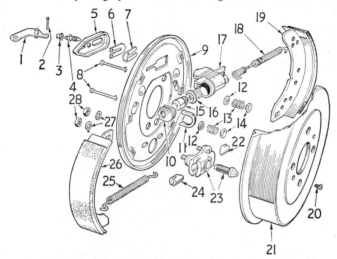

FIG. 38. TYPICAL REAR BRAKE ASSEMBLY, REMOVED FROM CAR AND
DISMANTLED

1. Handbrake lever	15. Piston
2. Split pin	16. Seal
3. Dust cap	17. Wheel cylinder
4. Bleed nipple	18. Return spring
5. Dust excluder	19. Brake shoe
6. Retaining clip	20. Countersunk screw
7. Retaining clip	21. Brake drum
8. Steady-pins	22. Adjuster tappet
9. Backplate	23. Adjuster wedge and body
10. Dust excluder	24. Adjuster tappet
11. Clip	25. Return spring
12. Steady-pin cups	26. Brake shoe
13. Springs	27. Shakeproof washers
14. Steady-pin cups	28. Nuts

adjuster, or the two adjusters, as the case may be, as far as possible. The drum can then be drawn off after the two countersunk securing screws have been removed.

Before removing the brake shoes it is as well to have handy some means of retaining the operating pistons in their cylinders. Otherwise, owing to the slight residual pressure that is maintained in the braking system, the pistons will tend to creep outwards, resulting in loss of fluid and entry of air into the system. Short lengths of wire or twine will serve or, better still, stout rubber bands cut from an old inner tube.

Disengage the cups and springs from the shoe steady-pins. The shoes and pull-off springs can then be removed by levering the tip of one shoe out of the operating fork. The shoes can then be collapsed together, allowing the pull-off springs to be unhooked and the shoes removed.

The backplate should be thoroughly cleaned with paraffin. If there is any evidence of leakage of oil or grease from the hub bearing, the oil seal must be renewed. Otherwise, the new linings will remain effective for only a short period. Similarly, it is false economy to attempt to clean

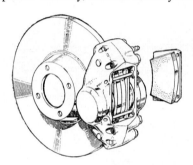

FIG. 39. FRONT DISC BRAKE CALIPER

Two types of brake pad are shown. The flange of the earlier type is cut away to take the pad-retaining pins. The later type is drilled and the pins passed through it. The two designs are not interchangeable.

oil-soaked linings with petrol or paraffin in an attempt to obtain a further period of service. Although the surfaces of the linings may appear to be in good condition after cleaning, the very high temperatures generated whenever the brakes are applied will liquefy the lubricant that has seeped down into the fibres of the friction material, and this will thus come to the surface.

It is also false economy to purchase cheap linings from a cut-price supplier, or to attempt to rivet new linings to the existing shoes without the use of an efficient lining clamp. The safest plan is to fit only factory-relined shoes.

The full benefit will not be obtained from new linings, of course, if the brake drums are badly scored. Unless the ridges are very deep, a specialist will be able to regrind the drums.

It is always a good plan to renew the pull-off springs when fitting replacement shoes, as weak springs can be a cause of brake judder or squeal. Some old hands recommend that the ends of the new linings should be bevelled-off, also with the object of preventing squeal or judder. This, however, has been proved to be a complete fallacy—bevelling the leading edges of the linings, in fact, is often apt to cause or contribute to these troubles, rather than cure them. The edges of the linings should be perfectly clean and square.

After the first few hundred miles, when the new linings have had an

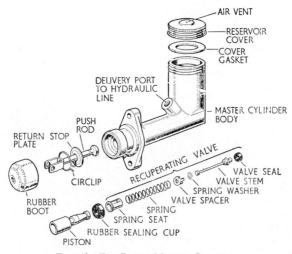

FIG. 40. THE BRAKE MASTER CYLINDER

opportunity to bed down, it will probably be possible to take up each adjustment by one or two clicks.

Renewing Disc Brake Friction Pads. On models fitted with disc brakes on the front wheels it is a simple matter to renew the friction pads in the brake calipers. Replacement pads, consisting of steel plates to which the friction linings are bonded, must be fitted when the linings are worn down to a thickness of about ⅛ in.

To remove the worn pads, jack up the front of the car and remove the wheels. The pads are retained by steel pins which are in turn held in place by spring clips. When the clips have been removed and the pins pulled out, the pads can be extracted. Clean away any mud, grit or rust from the caliper and push the operating pistons back into their bores before sliding in the new pads. Forcing the pistons inwards will raise the fluid level in the master cylinder reservoir. It is wise to syphon off some of the fluid, therefore, to prevent it overflowing. Make sure that the retaining pins are properly fitted and secured by the spring clips. Finally, pump the brake pedal until a solid resistance is felt. It is not necessary to bleed the braking system after fitting new pads, but remember to top-up the reservoir.

Servicing the Hydraulic Components. In view of the vital importance of the braking system and the serious consequences that may arise if a minor component in the hydraulic system should be assembled incorrectly, it should not be necessary to stress the advisability of entrusting the overhaul or repair of the master cylinder or wheel cylinders to a specialist.

It is not that the work itself entails any special difficulties: but the recognition of the degree of wear or deterioration of various parts that necessitates replacement calls for a certain amount of experience.

Long-term Maintenance. Brake manufacturers now recommend that the fluid should be drained from the system after about 24,000 miles or 18 months and replaced by fresh fluid.

The reason for this is that the fluid absorbs moisture from the air and this may eventually lead to the formation of steam in the wheel cylinders due to the very high temperatures that are generated under severe braking conditions. The result will be a serious—possibly total—loss of braking power. From this it also follows that hydraulic fluid should never be stored in any container which is open to the atmosphere.

After about 36,000 miles or 3 years in service is it a wise precaution to renew all the rubber parts in the system—the flexible hoses, piston cups and seals. At the same time the bores of the master cylinder and slave cylinders should be examined for any signs of corrosion or pitting. This job is best left to a Triumph dealer unless you have had experience of dismantling the hydraulic components.

6 The Electrical Equipment and Instruments

ROUTINE maintenance and adjustment of the electrical equipment calls for only an elementary knowledge of electricity. In fact, it is always advisable to enlist the aid of an expert auto-electrician when a fault develops which is beyond elementary first-aid measures, such as tightening a loose connection or renewing or insulating a broken or chafed lead, and to take advantage of the service-exchange scheme operated by Standard-Triumph dealers and Lucas service depots, under which a faulty component is replaced by a reconditioned, guaranteed unit at a fixed charge.

Negative-earth Systems. The Herald 13/60 and the 1200 from approximately March 1968, the later Vitesse 2000 and the Spitfire Mark 3, all have negative-earth electrical systems. In other words, the negative terminal of the battery is connected to the metal of the car, instead of the positive terminal as on earlier models. This change was introduced in order to bring the electrical systems of British vehicles into line with those used in most other countries of the world.

For some years to come there will therefore be both positive-earth and negative-earth cars in use in Britain and it is important to check that the correct polarity is maintained whenever the battery has been removed and refitted. Any electrical components which contain silicon diodes or transistors will be damaged if incorrectly connected. Typical examples are radios, electronic rev. counters, electronic ignition systems, automatic parking lamps and headlamps and headlamp dipping devices, and alternator charging systems.

Battery Servicing. The filler plugs should be kept clean and tight to prevent acid leakage and the battery and the surrounding parts, particularly the tops of the cells, must be clean and dry.

Occasionally the connections should be removed so that the contact surfaces can be examined and any corrosion scraped off. Before they are refitted they should be lightly smeared with petroleum jelly.

If the battery has to be removed from the car, remember, when replacing it, that the correct terminal must be earthed; the "live" terminal is connected by a short lead to the terminal on the starter solenoid switch. The cable clamping bolts should be tightened just sufficiently to retain the clamps on the terminals. Over-tightening is liable to distort or fracture the clamps. Similarly, the battery-retaining clamp nuts should be just sufficiently tight to prevent movement of the battery on its mounting.

Specific Gravity of the Electrolyte. The best indication of the state of the charge of the cells is the specific gravity of the electrolyte, which can

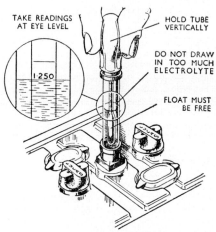

TAKE READINGS AT EYE LEVEL

HOLD TUBE VERTICALLY

DO NOT DRAW IN TOO MUCH ELECTROLYTE

1·250

FLOAT MUST BE FREE

FIG. 41. CHECKING THE SPECIFIC GRAVITY OF THE BATTERY ELECTROLYTE

TEMPERATE CLIMATES

Air temperature ordinarily below 90°F (32°C)

CONDITION OF CELL	HYDROMETER READING AT TEMPERATURE OF						
	50°F (10°C)	60°F (16°C)	70°F (21°C)	80°F (27°C)	90°F (32°C)	100°F (38°C)	110°F (43°C)
Fully charged .	1·288	1·284	1·280	1·276	1·272	1·268	1·264
Half charged .	1·208	1·204	1·200	1·197	1·193	1·189	1·186
Fully discharged	1·116	1·113	1·110	1·108	1·104	1·101	1·098

be ascertained by using a hydrometer. The readings for each of the cells should be approximately the same. A reading should not be taken immediately after adding distilled water, however; the battery should be

TROPICAL AND SUB-TROPICAL CLIMATES
(Note that the capacity of the battery is somewhat reduced since an acid of lower specific gravity is used)

CONDITION OF CELL	HYDROMETER READING AT TEMPERATURE OF						
	60°F (16°C)	70°F (21°C)	80°F (27°C)	90°F (32°C)	100°F (38°C)	110°F (43°C)	125°F (52°C)
Fully charged .	1·214	1·210	1·206	1·202	1·198	1·195	1·190
Half charged .	1·163	1·160	1·156	1·153	1·150	1·147	1·141
Fully discharged	1·102	1·100	1·097	1·093	1·090	1·087	1·083

charged for at least an hour to ensure that the water and acid are thoroughly mixed.

The electrolyte drawn into the hydrometer should be fairly clear; if it is dirty it is probable that the plates are in a bad condition, in which case a Standard-Triumph dealer or a battery agent should be consulted.

The specific gravity of the acid in the cells when fully charged should be within 0·005 (5 points) above or 0·010 (10 points) below the values given in the tables. The temperatures quoted are those of the electrolyte— not the prevailing atmospheric temperature at the time of the test.

Idle Batteries. A battery which is to stand idle should be charged at the normal charging rate of 4–4½ amperes until the specific gravity is within 0·010 of the fully charged value. Disconnect the wires from the battery to avoid loss of charge through any small leak in the wiring.

A battery not in active service may be kept in condition for immediate use by giving it a freshening charge at least once every two months. It should, preferably, also be given a thorough charge after an idle period before it is put into service. It is unwise to allow a battery that is in good condition to stand for more than two months without charging it.

THE CHARGING CIRCUIT

The charging rate of the generator, which is of the two-brush, compensated-voltage controlled type, is automatically regulated by a controller mounted on the engine bulkhead and depends on the state of charge of the battery, on the prevailing atmospheric temperature and on the load that is being imposed in the various circuits at any given moment. Thus the regulator automatically provides a large charging current when the battery is discharged, the rate being highest in cold weather; as the battery becomes charged the charging rate is reduced, tapering off to a "trickle" charge that keeps a fully-charged battery in good condition.

To prevent the battery discharging through the dynamo circuit whenever

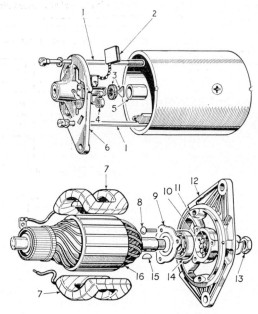

FIG. 42. TYPICAL GENERATOR

1. Bolts
2. Brush
3. Felt ring and aluminium sealing disc
4. Brush spring
5. Bearing bush
6. Commutator end-bracket
7. Field coils
8. Rivet
9. Bearing retainer plate
10. Corrugated washer
11. Felt washer
12. Driving end-bracket
13. Pulley retainer nut
14. Bearing
15. Woodruff key
16. Armature

the engine is stopped or is running at low speeds, an electro-magnetic switch—the cut-out—is combined with the regulator in the control box.

It is best to obtain expert advice if it is thought that the charging rate is too high or too low. The former will be indicated by the necessity for very frequent topping-up of the cells as the result of excessive "gassing" of the electrolyte; the latter by consistent under-charging of the battery. When adjusting the regulator, accurate voltage and amperage readings must be taken with high-grade moving-coil meters. This rules out make-shift methods of adjustment—which applies not only to the owner but also to a garage which does not have the necessary equipment. An incorrect setting of the regulator can quickly ruin the battery.

Ignition Warning Light. The red warning light incorporated in the speedometer dial should glow as soon as the ignition is switched on and when the engine is idling, but should fade out whenever the engine is speeded-up. If it continues to glow at normal running speeds, check for a slack or broken dynamo driving belt, especially if the light comes on suddenly during a spell of fast driving. As the belt also drives the fan and water pump, the sudden lighting-up of the warning lamp can enable one to spot the trouble before overheating occurs; a high reading on the engine temperature gauge (when fitted) might not be noticed until other symptoms of overheating had become evident.

If the driving belt appears to be sound and correctly tensioned, failure of the lamp to be extinguished indicates a fault in the charging circuit, either in the dynamo, control box or wiring, which should be investigated at the earliest possible opportunity by a specialist. The reserve of current stored in the battery can be exhausted comparatively quickly, particularly when driving at night—even if one forgoes the luxury of keeping the heater or radio in operation.

If the light does not glow when the ignition is first switched on, it is obviously essential to check the bulb in the warning lamp and renew it if necessary, or to trace and put right the fault in the circuit.

Home Charging. Many owners look on a home charger primarily as an insurance against occasional battery exhaustion, rather than as a useful aid to battery maintenance. But the relatively short life obtained from many modern batteries can often be ascribed to the heavy "boost" charge of up to 20 amperes which they receive when a car is driven away after a cold start. The correct normal charging rate for the battery is 4–4½ amperes.

Obviously, if a home charger is installed and the battery is kept at or near the fully charged condition, it will have a much easier life and the cost of the charger will eventually be more than saved; moreover, one has on the credit side the peace of mind that results from the certainty of an immediate start even on the coldest mornings.

THE GENERATOR

The routine maintenance of the generator is confined, as described in Chapter 1, to checking the tension of the driving belt every 6,000 miles and lubricating the rear bearing at 12,000-mile intervals by applying a few drops of engine oil to the hole in the bearing housing. Specialist attention

(say, at 12,000-mile intervals) entails inspection and cleaning of the commutator and brushes; it is preferable to leave this to a Standard-Triumph
dealer who will, at the same time, be able to check and if necessary adjust
the charging regulator.

THE STARTER MOTOR

Probably the most important of the auxiliaries that draw current from
the battery is the starter motor. Unlike the dynamo, it is in action only
intermittently and therefore normally has a long, trouble-free life;
because it requires no periodic lubrication it is, in fact, often overlooked
by the average owner. The starter should be serviced, however, at
reasonable intervals—say, every 12,000 miles—when it should be removed
from the car and dismantled by an expert, as in the case of the dynamo, so
that the commutator, brushes and the drive components can be inspected
and cleaned.

Testing the Starter. Assuming that the battery is in a charged condition,
the lights should be switched on during the test. If the lights go dim
although the starter does not operate, the indication is either that the
battery is discharged or that current is flowing through the windings but
for some reason the armature is not rotating, possibly because the pinion
is already engaged with the flywheel starter-ring.

If the lamps remain bright, however, the starter solenoid switch may be
faulty. It can be tested by pressing on the rubber cover over the plunger.
If the starter then operates, either the switch is not receiving current (it
will be necessary to check the dashboard switch and wiring) or the solenoid
switch is defective and must be replaced. If there is no response from the
starter when the switch plunger is firmly pressed, the cleanness and tightness of the terminals on the switch should be checked. A possible trouble
is burnt contacts within the switch, calling for renewal of the switch.

Freeing a Jammed Starter Pinion. If the starter pinion should become
jammed in mesh with the starter ring it can usually be freed by engaging
top gear and attempting to rock the car forward. It is a common mistake
to engage a lower gear and rock the car violently backwards and forwards; this usually jams the pinion more firmly in mesh and may damage
the drive.

If rocking the car forwards does not free the pinion, the small dust
cap on the end of the starter (if such a cap is fitted) should be removed
and the squared extension of the spindle should be rotated in a clockwise
direction with a spanner.

If Starter Does Not Engage. If the starter pinion does not engage with
the flywheel, the starter whirring idly, the starter drive probably requires
cleaning. It will be necessary to unbolt the starter from the engine,

supporting it from below. The pinion should move freely on the screwed sleeve; any dirt must be washed off with paraffin. A trace of paraffin should then be applied to the sleeve; oil must not be used owing to the risk of grit accumulating and causing the pinion to stick.

If the battery is discharged or weak, the starter may spin once or twice without engaging. This is a useful warning of future trouble that can result in one being stranded until a new battery or a tow is obtained.

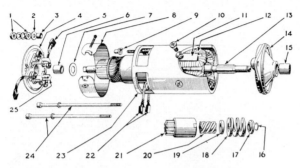

FIG. 43. STARTER MOTOR AND DRIVE

1. Terminal nuts and washers	14. End bracket
2. Insulating washer	15. Bush
3. Insulating bush	16. Jump ring
4. End plate	17. Retainer
5. Brush	18. Main spring
6. Bush	19. Thrust washer
7. Thrust washer	20. Sleeve
8. Cover band	21. Pinion and barrel assembly
9. Insulating bush	22. Brushes
10. Pole securing screw	23. Yoke
11. Pole piece	24. Through bolts
12. Field coil	25. Brush box
13. Shaft	

Starting in Winter. In very cold weather it may be an advantage to depress the clutch pedal to relieve the starter of the drag of the cold, thick oil in the gearbox. On the other hand, the friction of the clutch release bearing may be sufficient to slow down the cranking speed. It is advisable to make a test under both conditions. Operate the starter switch firmly and release it immediately the engine fires.

HEAD, SIDE AND REAR LAMPS

Except on models which are fitted with sealed-beam headlamp units, the headlamp reflectors are retained in position by three screws, access to which is obtained by slackening the small captive screw at the base of the headlamp rim, easing the rim upwards and outwards and taking off the dust-excluding rubber ring.

In addition to retaining the reflector, each screw acts as an adjustment for the direction of the headlamp beam. For example, screwing the uppermost screw inwards will tilt the reflector backwards and raise the

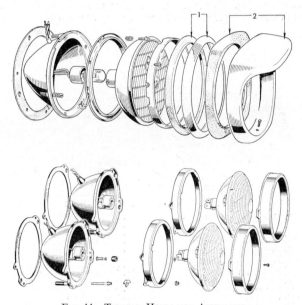

FIG. 44. TYPICAL HEADLAMP ASSEMBLIES

Above. Herald and Spitfire. The clip-on rim (1) is used on the Spitfire and the hooded rim (2) on the Herald. *Below.* Vitesse light-unit assemblies.

beam, whereas unscrewing it will lower the beam. Similarly, the two side screws enable the beam to be centralized or directed slightly to the left or right.

As a general rule, the headlamps should be adjusted so that when the main beam filaments are alight, the beams are parallel both to each other and to the ground. This will automatically give the correct position for the dipped beams. Allowance must be made, of course, for special conditions. For example, if the rear of the car is heavily loaded it will be necessary to lower the main beams slightly to avoid any risk of oncoming traffic being dazzled when the beams are in the dipped position. It will also be necessary to comply with any local regulations that may be in force. Remember, too, that as the bulbs age, the pre-focused filaments may sag and upset the focus and direction of the beams.

Renewing Headlamp Bulbs or Light Units. It is unnecessary to disturb the setting of the adjusting screws when removing the reflector and lamp glass unless the screws have been tightened to such an extent that it is impossible to rotate the reflector anti-clockwise when it has been pushed back against the resistance of the three springs, in order to allow the openings in the slots to register with the heads of the screws. In such a case the adjusting screws should be slackened-off and the headlamp should be realigned when the light unit has been replaced.

When sealed-beam light units are fitted no separate bulbs are used, the headlamp reflector and front lens forming, in effect, one large bulb. It will be necessary, therefore, to replace the unit if a filament should fail. First take off the cowl or the plated rim. On the Spitfire this simply snaps into place and is removed by inserting the end of a screwdriver behind the lower edge and levering sideways. Slacken or remove the three cross-headed screws that secure the retaining rim and withdraw the rim and the light unit. Do not disturb the two spring-loaded adjusting screws unless it is intended to reset the headlamp beam.

Side, Rear, Indicator, Panel and Roof Lamps. The lamp glass or cover of a side, rear or direction indicator lamp is retained by a screw or screws; the method of removal is self-evident.

In order to renew the panel or warning lamp bulbs the holders can be pulled out of their sockets at the back of the instrument panel, in which they are a light push fit.

ELECTRICAL ACCESSORIES

Under this heading we can group the windscreen wiper, horn and direction indicators.

Windscreen Wiper. The electrically-operated windscreen wiper normally requires no attention, other than renewal of the wiper blades at least once a year. Even blades that are in good condition cannot be effective, however, if the glass has acquired a coating of "traffic film," consisting largely of deposits caused by exhaust fumes (diesel-engined vehicles are particularly bad offenders in this respect) which result in persistent smearing of the raindrops in the path of the wiper blades. The silicones used in many modern car polishes can create a similar effect.

In either case the most satisfactory remedy is to clean the screen thoroughly with a liquid detergent, used undiluted. This should be of a non-bleaching type; the preparations sold for domestic washing-up purposes are excellent. Strong detergents may discolour the paintwork if allowed to remain on it for any length of time. In no circumstances should any abrasives be used as the glass is easily scratched. For the same reason, the wiper blades should not be kept in action on a dry screen.

If the blades do not sweep through satisfactory arcs or fail to park neatly, it is possible that at some time the arms have been incorrectly fitted to the driving spindles. No attempt should be made to rotate the arms while they are still attached to their spindles, as they engage with finely-cut splines that allow them to be accurately and positively positioned. Each arm must therefore be withdrawn by lifting a small retaining clip with the tip of a screwdriver and then refitted in the desired position.

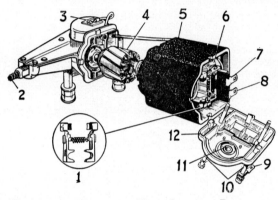

FIG. 45. THE WINDSCREEN WIPER PARTIALLY DISMANTLED

1. Brushgear assembly
2. Cable rack
3. Limit switch
4. Armature
5. Yoke
6. Field coil
7. Supply terminal "2"
8. Terminal "1" to switch
9. Earthing terminal "E"
10. Through-bolts
11. Self-aligning porous bronze bearing
12. Cover

Electric Horn. An adjustment is provided on the fixed contact of the horn but this is intended only to compensate for wear on the moving parts that takes place over a long period of use; it does not alter the note and should not normally be disturbed, as an ammeter should be used when making any adjustment; the maximum current drawn by each horn should not exceed 6 amperes.

When a horn fails to sound or becomes erratic in action, however, the trouble can most usually be traced to a loose or dirty contact or to a break in the wiring. An apparent change in the note, on the other hand, is usually caused either by loose mounting bolts (although the horn itself is flexibly mounted, the mounting bolts must be kept tight) or by sympathetic vibration of some component in the vicinity of the horn.

Flashing Indicators. The flashing indicator lamps are fed with inter-mittent current from a sealed control unit. This contains a switch which is actuated by the alternate expansion and contraction of a length of wire that is heated by the current passing to the indicator lamps, thus giving a flashing frequency of about 80–100 times per minute.

Failure or erratic action of the flashing indicators may be caused by dirty contacts in the indicator switch, in the wiring, or at the ignition switch terminal (indicated by failure also of the ignition warning light, fuel and temperature guages and other items fed from this terminal); or by a faulty flasher unit. While the former faults can be corrected by anyone with a little electrical knowledge, the flasher unit is not repairable. A replacement unit should be handled with care as it is a somewhat delicate component and can be out of action if it is dropped or receives a moderately hard knock.

FUEL AND TEMPERATURE GAUGES

The electro-magnetic fuel and temperature gauges fitted to all models except the Spitfire, estate cars and vans operate on similar principles. The panel unit contains two windings which produce separate magnetic fields; one winding sets up a constant pull on an armature attached to the pointer while the other, connected to the tank unit or the temperature bulb in the thermostat housing on the engine, as the case may be, pulls the pointer across the gauge dial to indicate the correct reading.

Fuel Gauge. The tank unit contains a contact blade that moves across a resistance as the float rises and falls. If the gauge becomes erratic or does not register, first make sure that current is reaching the B terminal on the dash unit when the ignition is switched on. Assuming that current is reaching the gauge, disconnect the tank unit lead. With the ignition switched on the pointer should now remain against the F mark. Next reconnect the lead to the gauge and earth the tank unit end. The pointer should then read E. If either test is unsuccessful the advice of a Standard-Triumph agent should be sought. The fault-tracing chart given on page 114 may, however, enable the trouble to be traced.

Temperature Gauge. The temperature bulb fitted into the thermostat housing at the front of the engine contains a pellet of material, the electrical resistance of which varies with changes in temperature. Should the gauge give trouble, check that current is reaching the gauge and that the wire between the gauge and the resistance element is sound, with clean, secure connections. The only practicable test is by substitution. If either the gauge or the temperature element is faulty a new unit must be fitted. Never connect either unit directly to the battery.

Thermal-type Gauges. The fuel gauge and temperature gauge of the Herald 13/60, the later Vitesse, the Spitfire, estate car and van operate on

(continued on page 114)

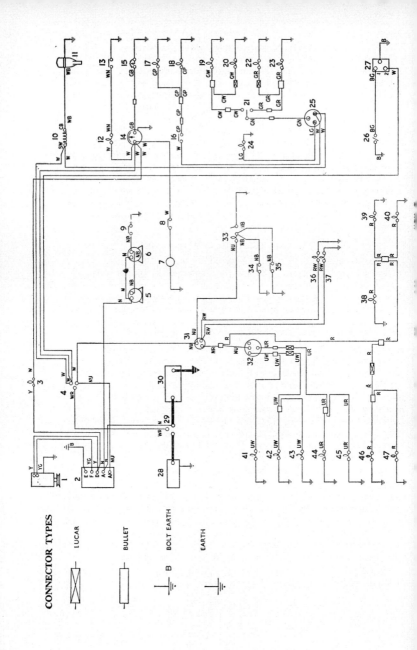

CONNECTOR TYPES

LUCAR

BULLET

B   BOLT EARTH

EARTH

Key to Fig. 46

Cable colour code

B. Black   K. Pink   Y. Yellow
U. Blue   P. Purple   D. Dark
N. Brown   R. Red   L. Light
G. Green   S. Slate   M. Medium
   W. White

1. Generator
2. Control box
3. Ignition warning light
4. Ignition/start switch
5. Horn
6. Horn
7. Heater motor
8. Heater switch
9. Horn push
10. Ignition coil
11. Distributor
12. Oil-pressure warning light
13. Oil-pressure switch
14. Fuel gauge
15. Fuel tank unit
16. Stop lamp switch

17. R.H. stop lamp
18. L.H. stop lamp
19. R.H. rear flasher
20. R.H. front flasher
21. Flasher switch
22. L.H. front flasher
23. L.H. rear flasher
24. Flasher warning light
25. Flasher unit
26. Screen wiper switch
27. Screen wiper motor
28. Starter motor
29. Starter solenoid switch
30. 12 volt battery
31. Master lighting switch
32. Lighting switch

33. Interior light
34. R.H. courtesy light switch
35. L.H. courtesy light switch
36. Panel illumination bulb
37. Panel illumination bulb
38. Number plate lamp
39. R.H. tail lamp
40. L.H. tail lamp
41. Main beam warning light
42. R.H. headlamp main beam
43. L.H. headlamp main beam
44. R.H. headlamp dip beam
45. L.H. headlamp dip beam
46. L.H. sidelamp
47. R.H. sidelamp

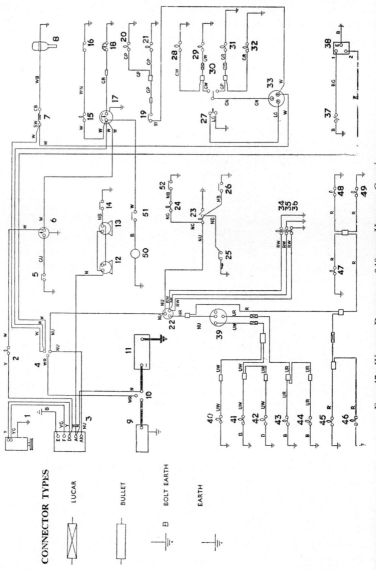

CONNECTOR TYPES

LUCAR

BULLET

B   BOLT EARTH

EARTH

Fig. 47. Wiring Diagram—948 c.c. Herald Coupé

Key to Fig. 47

The wiring of the Convertible is similar. Cable colour code as for Fig. 46

1. Generator
2. Ignition warning light
3. Control box
4. Ignition/starter switch
5. Temperature gauge transmitter
6. Temperature gauge
7. Ignition coil
8. Distributor
9. Starter motor
10. Starter solenoid switch
11. Battery
12. Horn
13. Horn
14. Horn switch
15. Oil-pressure warning light
16. Oil-pressure warning light switch
17. Fuel gauge
18. Fuel tank unit
19. Stop lamp switch
20. R.H. stop lamp
21. L.H. stop lamp
22. Master (lamps) switch
23. Interior light
24. Glove locker switch
25. L.H. courtesy switch
26. R.H. courtesy switch
27. Flasher warning light
28. R.H. rear flasher
29. R.H. front flasher
30. Direction indicator switch
31. L.H. front flasher
32. L.H. rear flasher
33. Flasher unit
34. Speedometer illumination bulb
35. Temperature gauge illumination bulb
36. Fuel gauge illumination bulb
37. Screen wiper switch
38. Screen wiper motor
39. Lighting switch (dip and side)
40. Main beam warning light
41. R.H. headlamp main beam
42. L.H. headlamp main beam
43. R.H. headlamp dip beam
44. L.H. headlamp dip beam
45. L.H. side lamp
46. R.H. side lamp
47. Number plate lamp
48. R.H. tail lamp
49. L.H. tail lamp
50. Blower motor
51. Heater switch
52. Glove locker light switch

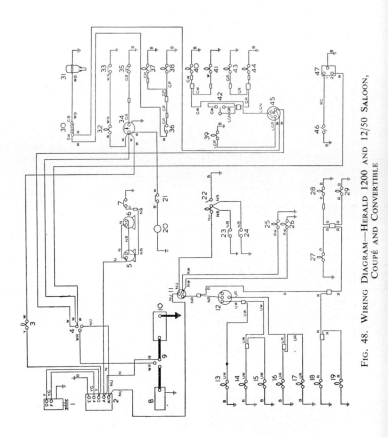

FIG. 48. WIRING DIAGRAM—HERALD 1200 AND 12/50 SALOON,
COUPÉ AND CONVERTIBLE

Key to Fig. 48

Cable Colour Code as for Fig. 46

1. Generator
2. Control box
3. Ignition warning light
4. Ignition/starter switch
5. Horn
6. Horn
7. Horn push
8. Starter motor
9. Starter solenoid switch
10. Battery
11. Master lighting switch
12. Column switch
13. Main beam warning light
14. R.H. headlamp main beam
15. L.H. headlamp main beam

16. R.H. headlamp dip beam
17. L.H. headlamp dip beam
18. L.H. side lamp
19. R.H. side lamp
20. Heater motor
21. Heater switch
22. Interior light and switch
23. R.H. courtesy light switch
24. L.H. courtesy light switch
25. Panel illumination
26. Panel illumination
27. Number plate lamp
28. R.H. tail lamp
29. L.H. tail lamp
30. Ignition coil
31. Distributor

32. Oil pressure warning light
33. Oil pressure warning light switch
34. Fuel gauge
35. Fuel tank unit
36. Stop lamp switch
37. R.H. stop lamp
38. L.H. stop lamp
39. Flasher warning light
40. R.H. rear flasher
41. R.H. front flasher
42. Flasher switch
43. L.H. front flasher
44. L.H. rear flasher
46. Screen wiper unit
47. Screen wiper motor

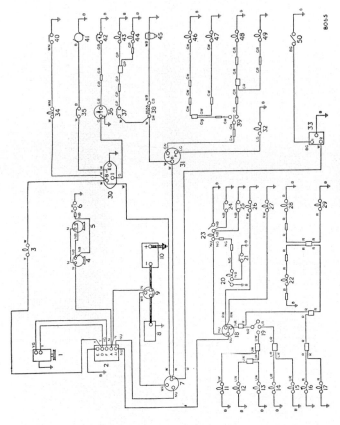

FIG. 49. WIRING DIAGRAM—HERALD 1200 ESTATE CAR AND COURIER

Key to Fig. 49

Cable Colour Code as for Fig. 46

1. Generator
2. Control box
3. Ignition warning light
4. Horn
5. Horn
6. Horn push
7. Ignition/starter switch
8. Starter motor
9. Starter solenoid
10. Battery
11. Main beam warning light
12. R.H. headlamp main beam
13. L.H. headlamp main beam
14. R.H. headlamp dip beam
15. L.H. headlamp dip beam
16. L.H. side lamp

17. R.H. side lamp
18. Master light switch
19. Column light switch
20. Tail gate light and switch
21. Tail gate switch
22. Number plate lamp
23. Interior light and switch
24. R.H. courtesy light switch
26. Panel illumination
27. Panel illumination
28. R.H. tail lamp
29. L.H. tail lamp
30. Voltage stabilizer
31. Flasher unit
32. Flasher warning light
33. Wiper motor
34. Oil pressure warning light

35. Heater switch
36. Fuel gauge
37. Stop lamp switch
38. Ignition coil
39. Flasher switch
40. Oil pressure switch
41. Heater motor
42. Tank unit
43. L.H. stop light
44. R.H. stop light
45. Distributor
46. R.H. rear flasher
47. R.H. front flasher
48. L.H. rear flasher
49. L.H. front flasher
50. Wiper switch

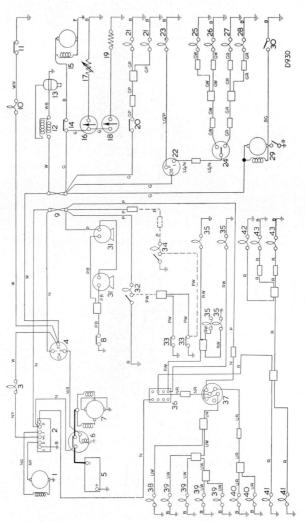

Fig. 50. Wiring Diagram—Vitesse Six

D930

Key to Fig. 50

Cable Colour Code as for Fig. 46

1. Generator
2. Control box
3. Ignition warning lamp
4. Ignition/starter switch
5. Battery
6. Starter solenoid
7. Starter motor
8. Horn push
9. Fuse unit
10. Oil pressure warning lamp
11. Oil pressure switch
12. Ignition coil
13. Distributor
14. Blower switch
15. Blower motor
16. Fuel gauge
17. Tank unit
18. Temperature gauge
19. Temperature transmitter
20. Brake stop lamp switch
21. Brake stop lamps
22. Flasher unit
23. Flasher monitor lamp
24. Direction indicator switch
25. Direction signal, R.H. front
26. Direction signal, R.H. rear
27. Direction signal, L.H. front
28. Direction signal, L.H. rear
29. Windscreen wiper motor
30. Windscreen wiper motor switch
31. Horns
32. Facia panel lamp[1]
33. Door-operated courtesy switch
34. Roof lamp[2]
35. Instrument illumination
36. Master lighting switch
37. Direction signal and headlamp flasher
38. Main beam warning lamp
39. Main beam lamps
40. Dipped beam lamps
41. Front parking lamps
42. Plate illumination lamp
43. Tail lamps

[1] The facia lamp is operated by the door courtesy switches (Convertible only).
[2] Not fitted on Convertible. On Saloon models the roof lamp is controlled by the courtesy switches.

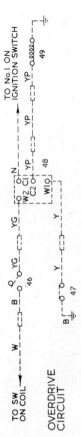

OVERDRIVE CONTROL CIRCUIT—VITESSE

46. Overdrive switch
47. Gearbox switch
48. Relay
49. Solenoid

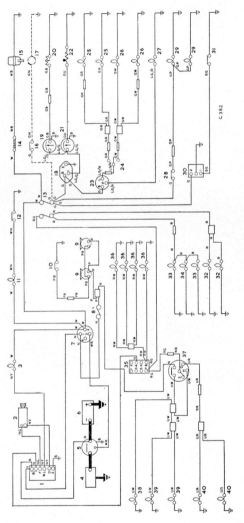

Fig. 51. Wiring Diagram—Spitfire

Key to Fig. 51

Cable Colour Code as for Fig. 45

1. Control box
2. Generator
3. Ignition warning lamp
4. Starter motor
5. Starter solenoid
6. Battery
7. Ignition/starter switch
8. Horn fuse
9. Horns
10. Horn push
11. Oil warning lamp
12. Oil pressure switch
13. Fuse unit
14. Ignition coil
15. Distributor
16. Heater blower switch*
17. Heater blower motor*
18. Voltage stabilizer
19. Fuel indicator
20. Fuel tank unit
21. Temperature indicator
22. Temperature transmitter
23. Flasher unit
24. Turn signal switch
25. Turn signal lamps L.H. side
26. Turn signal lamps R.H. side
27. Turn signal monitor
28. Brake/stop lamp switch
29. Brake/stop lamps
30. Windscreen wiper motor
31. Wiper motor switch
32. Front parking lamps
33. Tail lamps
34. Plate illumination lamps
35. Master lighting switch
36. Instrument illumination
37. Steering column light switch
38. Main beam warning lamp
39. Headlamp main beams
40. Headlamp dipped beams

* Special accessory

HORN CIRCUIT—FRANCE ONLY

1. Horn relay
2. Horn push
3. Switch
4. Fuse
5. Horn, l. h., low-note
6. Horn, r. h., high-note

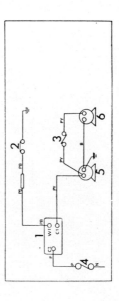

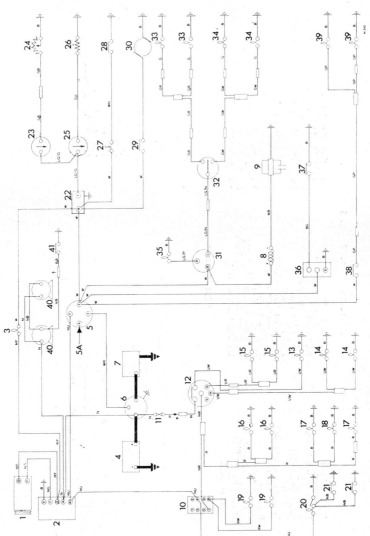

Fig. 52. Wiring Diagram—Herald 13/60

Key to Fig. 52

Cable colour code as for Fig. 46

1. Generator
2. Control box
3. Ignition warning light
4. Battery
5. Ignition/starter switch
5A. Ignition/starter switch—
    radio supply connector
6. Starter soleniod
7. Starter motor
8. Ignition coil
9. Ignition distributor
10. Master light switch
11. Line fuse
12. Column light switch
13. Main beam warning light
14. Main beam
15. Dip beam
16. Front parking lamp
17. Tail lamp
18. Plate illumination lamp
19. Instrument illumination
20. Facia lamp

21. Door switch
22. Voltage stabilizer
23. Fuel indicator
24. Fuel tank unit
25. Temperature indicator
26. Temperature transmitter
27. Oil pressure warning light
28. Oil pressure switch
29. Heater switch
30. Heater motor
31. Flasher unit
32. Flasher switch
33. L.H. flasher lamp
34. R.H. flasher lamp
35. Flasher warning light
36. Windscreen wiper motor
37. Windscreen wiper switch
38. Stop lamp switch
39. Stop lamp
40. Horn
41. Horn push

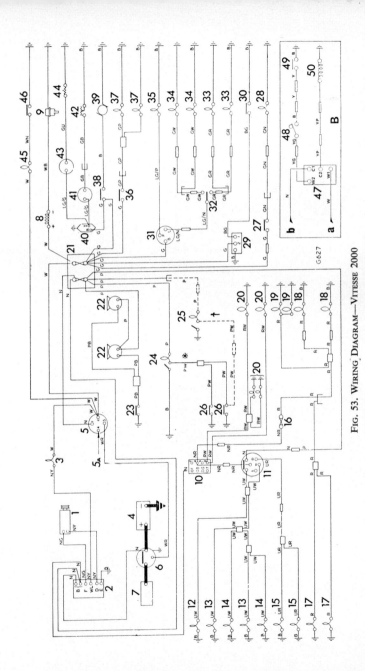

FIG. 53. WIRING DIAGRAM—VITESSE 2000

Key to Fig. 53

Cable colour code as for Fig. 46

1. Generator
2. Control box
3. Ignition warning light
4. Battery
5. Ignition/starter switch
5A. Ignition/starter switch—radio supply position
6. Starter solenoid
7. Starter motor
8. Ignition coil
9. Ignition distributor
10. Master light switch
11. Column light switch
12. Main beam warning light
13. Main beam—outer
14. Main beam—inner
15. Dip beam
16. Line fuse
17. Front parking lamp
18. Tail lamp
19. Plate illumination lamp
20. Instrument illumination
21. Fuse box
22. Horn

23. Horn push
24. Facia lamp
25. Roof lamp (saloon only)
26. Door switch
27. Reverse lamp switch
28. Reverse lamp
29. Windscreen wiper motor
30. Windscreen wiper switch
31. Flasher unit
32. Flasher switch
33. L.H. flasher lamp
34. R.H. flasher lamp
35. Flasher warning light
36. Stop lamp switch
37. Stop lamp
38. Heater switch
39. Heater motor
40. Voltage stabilizer
41. Fuel indicator
42. Fuel tank unit
43. Temperature indicator
44. Temperature transmitter
45. Oil pressure warning light
46. Oil pressure switch

50. Overdrive solenoid
a. From fuse box
b. From ignition/starter switch—connector 1

B overdrive (optional extra)

47. Overdrive relay
48. Overdrive column switch
49. Overdrive gearbox switch

Note: On convertible no roof lamp is fitted—door switches (26) control facia lamp (24). PW wire shown dotted and indicated * is fitted on convertible only.
On saloon door switches (26) control roof lamp (25). P and PW wire shown dotted and indicated † are fitted on saloon only.

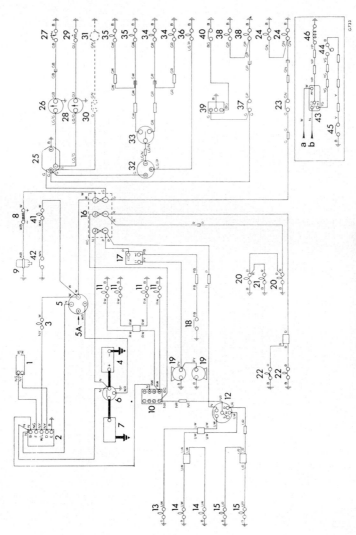

Fig 54. Wiring Diagram—Spitfire Mk 3

Key to Fig. 54

Cable colour code as for Fig. 46

1. Generator
2. Control box
3. Ignition warning light
4. Battery
5. Ignition/starter switch
5A. Ignition/starter switch—radio supply position
6. Starter solenoid
7. Starter motor
8. Ignition coil
9. Ignition distributor
10. Master light switch
11. Instrument illumination
12. Lights selector switch
13. Main beam warning light
14. Main beam
15. Dip beam
16. Fuse assembly
17. Horn relay
18. Horn push
19. Horn
20. Tail lamp
21. Plate illumination lamp
22. Front parking lamp
23. Reverse lamp switch
24. Reverse lamp
25. Voltage stabilizer
26. Fuel indicator

27. Fuel tank unit
28. Temperature indicator
29. Temperature transmitter
30. Heater switch (optional)
31. Heater motor (optional)
32. Flasher unit
33. Direction indicator switch
34. L.H. direction indicator lamp
35. R.H. direction indicator lamp
36. Direction indicator warning light
37. Stop lamp switch
38. Stop lamp
39. Windscreen wiper motor
40. Windscreen wiper switch
41. Oil pressure warning light
42. Oil pressure switch

OVERDRIVE (OPTIONAL)

43. Overdrive relay
44. Overdrive column switch
45. Overdrive gearbox switch
46. Overdrive solenoid
a. From ignition/starter switch—connector 2
b. From ignition/starter switch—connector 1

a different principle from the instruments just described. The pointer is deflected by a bi-metal strip which bends as it is heated by current passing through a coil which is wound around it. A small voltage regulator supplies the current to both gauges at a constant 10 volts and the amount of current flowing in each gauge is determined by the sliding resistance in the float-operated tank unit or by a temperature-sensitive pellet in the water-temperature transmitter bulb, as described earlier.

Fault-tracing with this type of gauge is confined to making sure that current is reaching the temperature regulator from the battery and that this unit is supplying the required 10 volts. If necessary, fit a replacement regulator, making sure that the B and E terminals are uppermost and are

SYMPTOM	CAUSE
Fuel gauge pointer remains at F	Disconnection in cable or terminals between gauge and tank unit
	Tank unit not earthed
	Faulty meter or tank unit
Pointer remains at E or does not move when ignition is switched on	Meter case not earthed
	Cable to tank unit short-circuited to earth
	Faulty meter or tank unit
	Lead from ignition switch to gauge disconnected
naccurate readings	Float arm on tank unit sticking
	Faulty gauge or tank unit

not more than 20 degrees from the vertical. If the gauge does not operate correctly with the replacement regulator installed, there is little that can be done, except to check the wiring between the gauge and the tank unit or the temperature transmitter, as the case may be, and then to substitute a serviceable unit at each point in turn until the culprit is isolated.

FAULT-TRACING AND FUSES

When it is necessary to carry out systematic fault-tracing, or when the time comes to renew all or part of the wiring, a detailed wiring diagram is, of course, invaluable. Systematic fault-tracing then becomes a matter of starting from the appropriate source of current and working progressively through the circuit until the fault is discovered.

No fuses are fitted to protect the various circuits on Herald models, except the 13/60, which has one line-fuse which protects the headlamp flasher circuit. This fuse is housed in a tubular container beside the ignition coil. On Spitfire and Vitesse models, the fuses are housed in clips in a fuse box mounted on the engine bulkhead.

7 Useful Facts and Figures

SOME of the information given here appears also in other chapters, but is repeated for quick reference when carrying out maintenance and adjustments.

Useful as these tables are, however, remember that car design is never static. Modifications are often introduced during the production run of a particular model and these may affect some of the figures given in the tables. If in doubt on any particular point, have a word with your local Standard-Triumph dealer. You will usually find him ready to give friendly advice.

Capacities (approx.)

	Fuel Tank	Cooling System
Herald 948 and "S"	7 Imp. gal (8½ U.S. gal, 32 litres)	8½ Imp. pints (10¼ U.S. pints, 4·8 litres)
Herald 1200, 12/50 and 13/60 Saloon .	6½ Imp. gal (7¾ U.S. gal, 29·6 litres)	8½ Imp. pints (10¼ U.S. pints, 4·8 litres)
Herald range Estate car, and Courier .	9 Imp. gal (10¾ U.S. gal, 41 litres)	8½ Imp. pints (10¼ U.S. pints, 4·8 litres)
Spitfire Mk 1 and 2	8¼ Imp. gal (10 U.S. gal, 36·7 litres)	9½ Imp. pints (11½ U.S. pints, 5·4 litres)
Spitfire Mk 3	8¼ Imp. gal (10 U.S. gal, 36·7 litres)	8 Imp. pints (9½ U.S. pints, 4·5 litres)
Vitesse 6	8¾ Imp. gal (10½ U.S. gal, 40 litres)	14 Imp. pints (16¾ U.S. pints, 7·4 litres)
Vitesse 2000 Mk 1 and 2 . . .	8¾ Imp. gal (10½ U.S. gal, 40 litres)	11 Imp. pints (13¼ U.S. pints, 6·2 litres)

Engine Oil (drain and refill), all models: 7 Imp. pints (8½ U.S. pints, 4 litres)
Rear Axle, all models: 1 Imp. pint (1¼ U.S. pints, 0·57 litre)
Gearbox, all models: 1½ Imp. pints (1¾ U.S. pints, 0·85 litre)
Gearbox, with overdrive, all models: 2⅜ Imp. pints (2⅞ U.S. pints, 1·35 litres)

Engine Specification

	Cylinder Bore	Crankshaft Stroke	Cubic Capacity	Compression Ratio (Standard)	Power Output (nett)	
					b.h.p.	at r.p.m.
Herald 948 and "S," Single-carburettor engine	62 mm (2·48 in.)	76 mm (2·992 in.)	948 c.c. (578 cu in.)	8·0:1	34·5	4,500
Twin-carburettor engine				8·5:1	45	5,800
Herald 1200 and Courier	69·3 mm (2·728 in.)	76 mm (2·992 in.)	1,147 c.c. (70 cu in.)	8·0:1	39	4,500
Herald 12/50	73·7 mm (2·9 in.)	76 mm (2·992 in.)	1,296 c.c. (79·2 cu in.)	8·5:1	51	5,200
Herald 13/60	6·93 mm (2·728 in.)	76 mm (2·992 in.)		8·5:1	61	5,000
Spitfire Mk 1		76 mm (2·992 in.)	1,147 c.c. (70 cu in.)	9·0:1	63	5,720
Spitfire Mk 2	73·7 mm (2·9 in.)	76 mm (2·992 in.)		9·0:1	67	6,000
Spitfire Mk 3			1,296 c.c. (79·2 cu in.)	9·0:1	75	6,000
Spitfire Mk 3 emission controlled	66·75 mm (2·628 in.)	76 mm (2·992 in.)		8·5:1	68	5,500
Vitesse 6	74·7 mm (2·94 in.)	76 mm (2·992 in.)	1,596 c.c. (97·39 cu in.)	8·75:1	70	5,000
Vitesse 2000 Mk 1			1,998 c.c. (122·0 cu in.)	9·5:1	95	5,000
Vitesse 2000 Mk 2				9·25:1	104	5,300

Number of cylinders: Herald and Spitfire models, 4; Vitesse models, 6.
Valve rocker clearances: All models 0·010 in. (0·25 mm), hot and cold.
Oil pressure: All models, 40–60 lb/sq in. (2·8–4·2 kg/sq cm) engine hot.

Carburettor

Herald 984 and "S",
   Single-carburettor engines   .   .   .   .   Single Solex B28 ZIC-2
   Twin-carburettor engines   .   .   .   Twin S.U. H1
Herald 1200, 12/50 and Courier   .   .   Single Solex B30 PSEI
Herald 13/60   .   .   .   .   .   Single Stromburg 150 CD
Spitfire Marks 1, 2 and 3   .   .   .   Twin S.U. HS2
Vitesse 6: Early engines   .   .   .   Twin Solex B32 PIH
   Engine Nos. HB6799–HB27985   .   .   Twin Solex B32 IH
   From engine No. HB27986   .   .   Twin Stromburg 150 CD
Vitesse 2000   .   .   .   .   .   .   Twin Stromburg 150 CD

Recommended Lubricants

Component	SAE Grade of oil
Engine, carburettor dampers and oil can . .	20W/50
Lower steering swivels, gearbox, rear axle . .	90 EP
and overdrive	
Front hubs, brake cables and grease gun . .	General-purpose grease
Clutch and brake reservoirs . . .	Castrol-Girling brake fluid (crimson)

Ignition System

	Sparking Plugs (Champion)	Ignition Timing, Standard Compression (see also pages 51–3)	Distributor
Herald 948 and "S,"			
Single carburettor	N–5	10° B.T.D.C.	Lucas
Twin carburettor	N–5	12° B.T.D.C.	Lucas
Herald 1200, 12/50 and Courier	L–87Y	15° B.T.D.C.	Up to engine No. GA67436 (Low comp). and GA86619 (High comp.), Lucas DM2 Later engines, Lucas 25 D4
Herald 13/60	N–9Y	9° B.T.D.C.	Lucas 25 D4
Spitfire Mark 1	L–87Y	13° B.T.D.C.	Delco-Remy D200
Spitfire Mark 2	L–87Y	17° B.T.D.C.	Delco-Remy D200
Spitfire Mark 3	N–9Y	6° B.T.D.C.	Delco-Remy D200
Vitesse 6	N–9Y	10° B.T.D.C.	Early engines, Lucas 25 D6 Engine No. HB15001–HB16301, Delco-Remy D200 From engine No. HB16302, Delco-Remy D202
Vitesse 2000. Mark 1	N–9Y	13° B.T.D.C.	Lucas 25 D6
Vitesse 2000, Mark 2	N–9Y	10° B.T.D.C.	Lucas 25 D6

Firing order: Herald and Spitfire models, 1,3,4,2; Vitesse models, 1, 5, 3, 6, 2, 4.
Sparking plug gap, all models: 0·025 in. (0·64mm)
Distributor contact-breaker gap, all models: 0·015 in. (0·4 mm)

Tyres

MODEL	Size	CONVENTIONAL (CROSS-PLY) Pressures, lb/sq in. (kg/sq cm)			RADIAL (BRACED-TREAD)	Pressures, lb/sq in. (kg/sq cm) All Conditions	
		Two-up Front	Two-up Rear	Fully laden Rear	Size	Front	Rear
Herald 13/60, 948 c.c., "S," 1200 c.c. (Saloon and Coupé), 12/50	5·20–13	19 (1·3)	24 (1·7)	28 (1·97)	145–13	22 (1·5)	27 (1·9)
Herald Estate Car	5·60–13	19 (1·3)	25 (1·76)	30 (2·1)	165–13	22 (1·5)	27 (1·9)
Herald Courier Van	5·60–13	15 (1·05)	25 (1·76)	32 (2·25)	—	—	—
with 6-ply tyres	5·60–13	15 (1·05)	25 (1·76)	36 (2·53)	—	—	—
Vitesse Six and 2000 Mk 1	5·60–13	22 (1·5)	24 (1·7)	26 (1·8)	165–13	24 (1·7)	26 (1·8)
Vitesse 2000 Mk 2	—	—	—	—	155SR–13	24 (1·69)	26 (1·83)
Spitfire	5·20–13	18 (1·27)	24 (1·7)	—	145SR–13	21 (1·47)	26 (1·8)

Notes: 1. When the Spitfire is to be used at sustained speeds in excess of 90 m.p.h. or is tuned to increase its maximum speed, radial-ply tyres should be used. For racing, consult the tyre company regarding the need for tyres of full racing construction.
2. For all models, to ensure good steering the relative differences in pressures between front and rear tyres must be maintained.
3. For sustained high-speed cruising, increase pressures by 6 lb/sq in. (0·42 kg/sq cm).
4. Adjust pressures only when tyres are cold.
5. For radial-ply tyres, confirm correct pressures from manufacturer's list of recommendations.

Dimensions (approx.)

	Overall Length	Overall Width	Overall Height	Ground Clearance (Static Laden)	Wheelbase	Turning Circle
Herald 948, "S," 1200, 12/50, 13/60 and Courier	12 ft 9 in. (389 cm)	5 ft 0 in. (152 cm)	4 ft 4 in. (132 cm)	6¾ in. (17 cm)	7 ft 7½ in. (233 cm)	25 ft (762 cm)
Spitfire Mk 1 and 2	12 ft 1 in. (369 cm)	4 ft 9 in. (145 cm)	3 ft 11½ in. (121 cm)	5 in. (12·5 cm)	6 ft 11 in. (211 cm)	24 ft (732 cm)
Spitfire Mk 3	12 ft 2½ in. (372 cm)					
Vitesse 6	12 ft 9 in. (389 cm)	5 ft 0 in. (152 cm)	4 ft 4 in. (132 cm)	6¾ in. (17 cm)	7 ft 7½ in. (233 cm)	25 ft (762 cm)
Vitesse 2000	12 ft 9 in (389 cm)	5 ft 0 in. (152 cm)	4 ft 5½ in. (136 cm)	5½ in. (14 cm)	7 ft 7½ in. (233 cm)	25 ft. (762 cm)

Track. Herald models: Front and rear, 4 ft 0 in.
Spitfire and Vitesse models: Front, 4 ft 1 in; Rear, 4 ft 0 in.

Weights, including Fuel, Oil and Water (approx.)

Herald 948 and "S"		15¾ cwt (800 kg)
Herald 1200 and 12/50, Saloon		16 cwt (810 kg)
Coupé		15¾ cwt (800 kg)
Convertible		16⅝ cwt (846 kg)
Estate car		16⅞ cwt (860 kg)
Courier		16¼ cwt (826 kg)
Herald 13/60, Saloon		16¾ cwt (851 kg)
Convertible		16¼ cwt (826 kg)
Estate car		17¾ cwt (900 kg)
Spitfire Mark 1 and 2		14 cwt (710 kg)
Spitfire Mark 3		14¾ cwt (748 kg)
Vitesse 6		18¼ cwt (927 kg)
Vitesse 2000		18¼ cwt (927 kg)

Index